FINDING FREEDOM

A Personal Exodus from Deception to Identity

Cassie Hutton

Copyright © 2018 Cassie Hutton

All rights reserved. No part of this publication may be reproduced, distributed, or transmitted in any form or by any means, including photocopying, recording, or other electronic or mechanical methods, without the prior written permission of the publisher, except in the case of brief quotations embodied in reviews and certain other non-commercial uses permitted by copyright law.

ISBN: 978-1-7908-4060-1

DOWNLOAD YOUR FREE COPY!

Just to say thanks for buying this book I would like to give you

"The Counterbalance: How to Respond and not React to the Spiritual Battle"

To download go to:
https://www.cassiehutton.com

Sign up for the email list and you will automatically receive your FREE copy in your inbox

Dedication

Galen- my husband, my best friend, and the one who keeps me sensible when this kite tries to fly higher than her strings will allow her to go. You are my anchor and my encourager. I love you!

My family- you kept me hopeful during this process even when you didn't know you were. Especially to Kelly and the Hutton family. You were so patient with me in my journey to accepting Christ. Thank you for not being judgmental and overbearing. You have always been open and you gently pointed me to the path of Truth. Thank you!

Thank you to my three boys, Trenton, Cole, and Cason. You were merciful and loving even on the days that I buried my face in this book all day long. You three are my greatest joy!

To Wendy, Jennifer, and Leslie who spent endless hours editing and proofreading to help me bring this book to life!

Lastly, thank you to everyone that planted a seed in my heart along my journey to finding freedom in Jesus Christ. Not every name is mentioned here but you know who you are. Everyone at Calvary Baptist Church in Gladewater, TX, and Bethesda Church in Lindale. You have helped shape me into the woman of God I am today. Thank you!

Table of Contents

Dedication .... *v*

Preface .... *ix*

Introduction: A Time for Jubilee *1*

Chapter 1: The Appointment *7*

Chapter 2: Growing in Deception *11*

Chapter 3: The Choice *19*

Chapter 4: Festering Wounds *27*

Chapter 5: Night Terrors *31*

Chapter 6: Promiscuous Girl *37*

Chapter 7: A Shift *43*

Chapter 8: Marriage & Family *53*

Chapter 9: Murder in the Parking Lot *61*

Chapter 10: Chaos *69*

Chapter 11: My Chains Are Gone *77*

Chapter 12: Spirit of Error *91*

Chapter 13: Adoption *103*

Chapter 14: My Freedom Walk *109*

Chapter 15: Surrendering the Secret *117*

Chapter 16: Deep Calls Out *121*

Preface

"I will answer them before they even call to me. While they are still talking about their needs, I will go ahead and answer their prayers!" - Isaiah 65:24 The Passion Translation (TPT)

The day the Lord told me to begin writing this book I was in my kitchen sweeping the floor. My three boys were getting older and I found myself with less to do around the house. I was getting bored and feeling a little lost during the day. Don't get me wrong, with a three-, four-, and five-year-old at home, I was plenty busy keeping up with them, but lately I found myself getting burned out. I enjoy restoring furniture but at the time I didn't have many projects to work on. I also make and sell homemade hot sauce, but neither of these are something I enjoy doing all the time. As I was sweeping, I remember saying, "Lord, I need something else to do that I love." Immediately, I heard Him say, "What about the book?"

I knew from the very beginning of my walk with Jesus that I was commissioned to "GO, and share my testimony." He spoke that to me in an audible voice. About two years after committing my life to Christ, He called my husband and me out of the Baptist church we were in and into a non-denominational church about forty minutes from our home.

Within two weeks of that move, I received two words of knowledge about books. The Lord told me to keep writing and journaling, and that I had a writer's anointing. This was very true. However, I had actually quit journaling as I had in the beginning. I had always loved to journal and write down everything the Lord gave me. I wrote down visions, dreams, words, or testimonies of His amazing orchestration of events and power. Somewhere along the way though, I became very discouraged. I figured, "what's the point?" I shut down and started going through the motions. I still wanted more of the Lord and what He had for my husband and me but as far as writing down what He gave me, I just abandoned it. I kept it to myself and maybe two or three other people. I justified it by thinking that this "writer's desire" was just my selfish ambition and there were already too many books in the world for me to write another one.

What a lie!

Once the Lord told me to go ahead and begin writing the book, I had a sudden desire to write whereas before I just knew I would someday. I suddenly had not just a plan to write but an inner passion that began to burn to see this book birthed.

If you have even the slightest desire to write, let this be your wake-up call. WRITE!

Introduction:

A Time for Jubilee

"And ye shall hallow the fiftieth year, and proclaim liberty throughout all the land unto all the inhabitants thereof: it shall be a jubilee unto you; and ye shall return every man unto his possession, and ye shall return every man unto his family." – Leviticus 25:10 King James Version (KJV)

Freedom is something every human being desires. Freedom is the essence of our spiritual longing. It is liberty, it is deliverance, and it is the state of not being imprisoned or enslaved. There are both physical and spiritual freedoms. When the spirit finds freedom, physical bondage loses its power and control. Aside from love, I believe it is possibly the greatest desire we have. True love is the power to set us free. 1 John 4:8 says "God is love."

America was founded for the sake of our freedom. Our forefathers wanted freedom from King George III's oppressive rule over the people.

Even our pets and animals long for freedom. If you've ever kenneled your dog, it leaps with joy the moment you open the cage. It will jump, bark, run, and play until its energy is exhausted. I grew up with horses, and many times I had to keep them stalled. When I was in college, that's all I could find for boarding. I remember making time to turn them out of their stalls. I would fling the gates wide open and they would take off running, bucking, playing, and enjoying every second of their freedom! It was one of the most enjoyable things I did while I was in college. I looked forward to it. Watching them play and enjoy their freedom was liberating even for me. I got to stop time just for those few moments every afternoon; where class assignments and tests were not on the agenda, where the evening sun and the bird's song became my study, where my mind stopped spinning and all people, papers, and problems no longer existed.

freedom | free·dom | ˈfrē-dəm

The world's definition of freedom, according to Merriam-Webster's Online Dictionary[1], is:

1. The quality or state of being free: such as
   a) The absence of necessity, coercion, or constraint in choice or action
   b) Liberation from slavery or restraint or from the power of another: independence
   c) The quality or state of being exempt or released usually from something onerous (freedom from care)
   d) Unrestricted use

In the New Testament, there are eight different Greek words that translate to "liberty," but I want to look at only one and gain a Biblical understanding of "jubilee" freedom. The Greek word aphesis[2] (ä'-fe-sēs) is used 16 times in the New Testament but is translated as the English word "liberty" only once.

---

[1] Freedom. 2018. In Merriam-Webster.com. Retrieved September 15, 2018, from *https://www.merriam-webster.com/dictionary/freedom*

[2] G859 - aphesis - Strong's Greek Lexicon (KJV). Retrieved from *https://www.blueletterbible.org//lang/lexicon/lexicon.cfm?Strongs=g859&t=kjv*

Finding Freedom

"Aphesis" is defined by Strong's Lexicon as "from the root word aphieme meaning freedom; (fig.) pardon: deliverance, forgiveness, liberty, remission." The only time this word is used in context of being released from bondage or imprisonment is in Luke 4:18:

> **"The Spirit of the Lord is upon me, because he hath anointed me to preach the gospel to the poor; he hath sent me to heal the brokenhearted, to preach deliverance *(aphesis)* to the captives, and recovering of sight to the blind, to set at liberty *(aphesis)* them that are bruised." - Luke 4:18 KJV**

"Aphesis" is used twice in this verse. In the other 15 times it is used in the New Testament, it is translated remission or forgiveness of sins. It doesn't just mean partial forgiveness, it means a "total pardon of sins (properly, the letting them go, as if they had not been committed), remission of their penalty."[3] For example, in Acts 2:38, the word is rendered:

> **"Then Peter said unto them, Repent, and be baptized every one of you in the name of Jesus Christ for the remission *(aphesis)* of sins, and ye shall receive the gift of the Holy Ghost." – Acts 2:38 KJV**

There are also Old Testament truths that give additional insight into these ideas of freedom and liberty:

---

[3] G859 - aphesis - Strong's Greek Lexicon (KJV). Retrieved from *https://www.blueletterbible.org//lang/lexicon/lexicon.cfm?Strongs=g859&t=kjv*

"The Spirit of the Lord GOD is upon me; because the LORD hath anointed me to preach good tidings unto the meek; he hath sent me to bind up the brokenhearted, to proclaim liberty to the captives, and the opening of the prison to them that are bound." - **Isaiah 61:1 KJV**

Isaiah 61:1 is the verse Jesus read in the synagogue to his hometown in Luke 4:18. And in Luke 4:21 Jesus tells them, "The scripture you've just heard has been fulfilled this very day! If we take a closer look at the Hebrew word for liberty, we get another take on it. The Hebrew word for liberty in Isaiah 61 is dᵉrôwr, (der-ore'). It comes from "an unused root (meaning to move rapidly); freedom; hence, spontaneity of outflow, and so clear: liberty, pure."[4] It's a flowing of pure life. Five out of the seven times dᵉrôwr is used in the King James, the word "proclaim" precedes "liberty". There is an understanding to declare publicly and to announce or preach – to proclaim – that freedom is here and the time is now! The second time the Hebrew word dᵉrôwr is mentioned, and the first time it is translated "liberty,"[5] is in Leviticus:

---

[4] H1865 - dĕrowr - Strong's Hebrew Lexicon (KJV). Retrieved from https://www.blueletterbible.org//lang/lexicon/lexicon.cfm?Strongs=H1865&t=KJV

[5] dĕrowr - Strong's Hebrew Lexicon (KJV). Retrieved from https://www.blueletterbible.org//lang/lexicon/lexicon.cfm?Strongs=H1865&t=KJV

"And ye shall hallow the fiftieth year, and proclaim liberty *(dᵉrôwr)* throughout all the land unto all the inhabitants thereof: it shall be a jubilee unto you; and ye shall return every man unto his possession, and ye shall return every man unto his family." – Leviticus 25:10 KJV

This is when the Lord established The Year of Jubilee. In a Jubilee year, the Lord commanded His people to blow the trumpet to proclaim freedom throughout the land. It was a time to let the land rest, to forgive debts owed to one another, and to set their slaves free (Leviticus 25:40-41). It was a time for everyone and everything to be restored back to their original destiny. The land was returned to its original owner and everyone returned to their family's land. The Year of Jubilee only occurred every fifty years, following the Day of Atonement. The Lord promised His people that if they would follow these commands, He would bless them.

The Year of Jubilee wasn't just for the one who still owed debts and was a slave to his master. It was also for the freeman, the one who didn't owe anyone anything. He had to let his slaves go. He had to release everything as well. The Year of Jubilee was a time for forgiveness to be both received and given! It was a time for "suddenlies." As soon as the trumpet blasted, the time for freedom was at hand. Jubilee is a time for great celebration!

The Old Testament is a type and shadow of what Jesus came to fulfill. When He proclaimed to his hometown that He came to fulfill the prophecy written by Isaiah, the fulfillment of the Year of Jubilee had come! It has come and is still here! Freedom is here to set the captives free, so we will no longer be bound by sin and demons. Because Jesus is our Jubilee, you can be delivered from addiction, fear, worry, anxiety, guilt, and shame. He is the chain breaker over these things that have you bound. The Blood of the Lamb is the fulfillment of the Law and is the only source of power needed to set you free from the chains holding you down. The true Lamb of God has come to be the once-for-all-time sacrifice for every sin you and I have ever committed!

> **"And he has entered once and forever into the Holiest Sanctuary of All, not with the blood of animal sacrifices, but the sacred blood of his own sacrifice. And he alone has made our salvation secure forever."**
> **– Hebrews 9:12 TPT**

That's what freedom is for us, too – it is a celebration of the separation from every worldly thing that holds us back. We celebrate the breaking free of the chains and pressures this world puts on us. We celebrate freedom from the worldly pressures of the corporate ladder. We celebrate freedom from strife, oppression, depression, heaviness, greed, lust, poverty, jobs, and redundancy. The list goes on and on. You could add your own thing to this list. The truth is, you can be set free from all of these things even if they still have to be in your life. Once you're set free from them, they no longer control you. It's no longer your heart's pilgrimage or the spinning wheel in your mind.

Freedom is an ongoing, lifelong process. But once you find it, you only want more of it!

Chapter 1:

The Appointment

I can barely remember the most significant day of my life. Thirteen years later, only bits and pieces come to me in snapshots as I try to recall that day. It was a summer day in late July or early August. I remember this much, because I had told my mom about this day at the youth rodeo in Shawnee, Oklahoma a month earlier. This day probably would have happened sooner if the summer hadn't been so busy between my high school rodeos and my brother's baseball games. My little brother, who is four years younger than me, qualified for the Little League World Series in Minnesota that summer (not Dixie League).

Due to my circumstances, I chose to fly home early from Minnesota and make an excuse that I missed my boyfriend, Tony (not his real name). One of the most memorable times and greatest achievements of my brother's life and here I was choosing to go home. I missed most of their games and a trip to Niagara Falls. They ended up 16th overall that year and I know they played their hearts out! It was a trip of a lifetime. We met Muhammed Ali, watched him throw the opening pitch that year before the games began, and even got his autograph from the door of his motorhome. He was already very sick with Parkinson's disease, but he mustered up enough energy to continue entertaining the crowds! They played his famous saying as he walked out onto the field, "Float like a butterfly, sting like a bee!" It was a day to remember and I didn't realize the significance of it until much later in life.

I flew home and started making plans.

Finally, the day had arrived. I don't remember what the weather was like. I don't remember how I really felt. By this time I had learned to stuff my emotions, not talk about what I was about to do. Nobody wanted to talk about it, we went with what was "best." I don't remember waking up that morning, getting dressed, or getting in the truck. I remember riding in the back seat of a gray three-quarter-ton Dodge pickup. I turned on a CD by Colby Yates called "Headed to The Rodeo." My boyfriend was sitting in the backseat with me and his dad was driving through Dallas traffic. I don't even remember if the roads were busy. I don't know what time of day it was. I don't remember driving into the parking lot or even getting out of the truck.

The second memory I have of that day is walking up a flight of stairs to a police officer standing outside the door in the hallway. He had a clipboard in his hand.

As Tony and I approached the officer he asked for my name. He checked my name off on the list fastened to the clipboard.

Then, he questioned, "What's the password?"

"Hamburger," I replied.

He opened the door and we walked in. I checked in at the counter, peed in a cup, sat and waited. The room was packed with people. I remember looking over at a couple with rings on their fingers. It was a young black couple that sat very quietly with their heads down. Shame was written all over them.

All I could think was, "What are married couples doing here?" Before long, a blonde girl came stumbling out the side door, legless and out of her right state of mind. Just a few minutes earlier I saw her go back and she was completely sober! What happened to her? The lady that I assumed was her mother walked her out the door and she was gone.

At some point they called my name. The next thing I can remember is sitting in a small office with Tony and a young, brunette lady asking me some questions.

"When was your last period?"

"How are you going to pay today?"

We weren't in her office very long. She asked some basic questions and that was it. I continued to stuff down what I was really feeling so I could get through with this "procedure." Get it over with. Quit thinking about it! The only response I remember giving this lady – being 17 at the time – I felt the need to tell her that I never had "anything" done. By "anything" I meant that I had never been to see a gynecologist. I don't know why that was so important at the time, but it was something that kept rolling through my mind. We paid the three hundred plus dollars and Tony went back to the waiting room, while I was sent to the exam room.

Ironically, two months prior to this day, in my summer high school credit class at a local community college, I had written a paper on why abortion was wrong. Two months ago, I never imagined I would be in a building called Planned Parenthood. Two months ago, I was reading all the statistics and what happens when a woman has an abortion. They vacuum the fetus out. The vacuum is 29 times stronger than a regular household vacuum. Two months ago, I couldn't imagine why anyone would ever consider such a horrendous act. Taking the very thing that's growing inside of you and sucking it out? How could anyone argue that it wasn't wrong?

When I first found out I was pregnant I didn't want to "get rid of it." But after a few weeks my mind just couldn't wrap around an actual baby. I couldn't see myself being a mother. Plus, how would I support this child? It seems selfish now, but more than anything, I wanted a good future and to finish my senior year of varsity volleyball. I knew I could go on to play college ball. Abortion had to be the best choice. Just get rid of the problem. It will all go away.

Somehow, I didn't consider this child as a life. All I knew was the pregnancy test was positive. "I'm pregnant," but what does that really mean? How far along was I? How big was this thing growing inside me? I definitely felt different. Physical changes were happening that I had never experienced before. But an actual baby? I could not wrap my mind around it! It didn't feel like a baby. I couldn't see myself being a mom at 17. My whole future was ahead of me. Varsity volleyball, rodeos, college, friends. How was I going to make money if I couldn't go to college? All the things the world tells you and everything I had "learned" in school was beginning to control my thoughts and emotions. Abortion couldn't really be that bad. It was an option, and an option I was willing to choose.

Chapter 2:

Growing in Deception

Growing up, horses, rodeos, barrel racing, and sports were a way of life for my family. My stepdad, Bill, was always willing to coach us at any of our baseball games and my mom loved to barrel race. It was really all I knew. I had three other siblings: a step brother and sister who were older than me and one younger brother that my stepdad and mom had after they were married. We all grew up playing sports and riding horses.

Being the only child that didn't biologically belong to my stepdad, I felt left out, different, or treated unfairly many times. I was very scared of Bill when I was younger. I was a sensitive child and hated any conflict or confrontation. I was especially intimidated by Bill. As I got older our relationship grew volatile at times but eventually I grew to love the man he was and appreciated the love he had for all of his children.

My mom, Pam, is a very gentle soul and I get my sensitivity from her. She eats, sleeps, and breathes horses. She has ever since she was a young girl and that has never changed. She took us to a barrel race almost every weekend growing up and I always had a good horse to ride. The first time I won anything "big" in barrel racing was at the Josey Ranch in Karnack, Texas. I was eleven years old in May 1998 and for the first time, I was entered at the Josey World Champion Junior Barrel Race. It was a big deal, kind of a rite of passage for young barrel racers. Everyone wants to compete at Josey's! I made it to the short go and placed 10th. Just good enough to win a saddle! My back number that year was 111 and I ended up winning $1,111 after the weekend was over. It was such a strange "coincidence", but I grew to really like the number 11. Anytime I had a chance to choose my own number in sports, I chose 11. Or, I would make it a big deal if I drew a number 11 in a game, or was 11th in line. Anytime 1's showed up, I was excited!

It's funny now but after that year, barrel racing became more of a hard game of strategy than it did fun. I started hitting barrels, getting nervous before I ran about hitting barrels, it became more than just a fun time. It became nerve-racking. But I didn't want to give it up, and I didn't. That next year I went on to win Rookie of the Year in the United Professional Rodeo Association. I qualified for the short-go at the Josey Junior World once again and would have ended up even higher in the standings but I hit a barrel that year. I made it back to the short-go at a big barrel race in Oklahoma City as well, but hit a barrel. I always had "beginners luck" but nothing ever seemed to stand and last a long time. Horses ended up dying from crazy diseases. The veterinarians would say they had "never seen something like this before" to numerous of our horse's cases. One year it seemed like we would never have another horse worth anything again. I even had one stolen right from our trailer, and never found him!

After that year, when I turned 12, I have a distinct loss of memory of happy times, fun times, and a stress-free life. There is a richness to my memories before that age. After 12, my memory is dull of the colorful and meaningful times I had with family, friends, activities, and life. Even in this moment, writing this part of my story, I am saying, "Lord, restore those years and bring back to my remembrance the happy times!" I know they are there. Nothing changed, so why do I have that distinct memory loss? John 10:10 tells us that the enemy comes to steal, kill, and destroy, but Jesus came so that we could have abundant life!

Lies were being planted in me at a very strategic time and I was easy bait. I didn't have any spiritual protection, I was vulnerable. I didn't have a strong daddy figure, and I was about to hit the teenage years of hormonal change and peer pressure. What better target?

By the time I was a young teenager, I thought I knew it all, had seen it all, and could make it in life. When you're young, you have such a small view of life. You're supposed to grow up, go to college, get a job, and raise a family. That's the way it works. I believed that, and I really wanted it. But I also wanted things I wasn't ready for.

I experienced things with girls at a very young age. Probably before I was even ten, I "experimented" with one girl in particular. We would make out and pretend that each other was the boyfriend. There were many times we did more than just make out. We would even pretend we were in bed with a guy. I already had two sexual relationships by the time I was 15 and the last one was very unhealthy. I had a best friend that I loved to go out and party with. We would even kiss each other because we knew the guys liked it to some extent. We always got all kinds of attention and cheers when we did it.

My second relationship was with a guy who was four or five years older than me. I was only 15 so that put him around 20. During that year-and-a-half relationship, he would belittle my family and me. I believed I wasn't good enough, that he was the "best thing" for me; and every time he got mad I thought that somehow, some way I could have done something different. I could have done something to change the outcome so he wouldn't have gotten so angry at me. Somehow every fight was truly my fault. Eventually, he moved out of the state and broke up with me. Deep down, I think he knew that he was really hurting me and that he wasn't healthy for me. It took him truly leaving for me to let him go.

Shortly after that relationship ended, another one began, followed by a third serious relationship when I was 16.

I know now this is actually a generational curse in my family. Exodus 34:7 tells us how iniquities get passed down the generations in families. This is something that happens to every one of my family members. We break up with one just to move to the next, both men and women. Those cycles must be broken, and I encourage you to study up on generational curses if you have family members participating in unhealthy, unrighteous behaviors. Ask Holy Spirit for the root of where this door was opened in your family lineage. The iniquities of our fathers must be repented for, and you will notice a huge shift in your family if you will only repent for them.

This was the first time I dated someone my own age. All the other guys were at least three to five years older than me. I don't know that I truly liked Tony, but there is something about someone liking you, admiring you, saying sweet things to you, and giving you lots of attention that causes some girls to just give in, especially when you don't have a strong, loving male figure or father in your life. Knowing you're admired and loved and the center of someone's attention causes you to be blind to what you really want. That weakness causes you to give in to what others want and you start to believe what they say to you. It's unhealthy in every way but I couldn't see that at the time.

I met Tony at a high school rodeo. He lived about three hours from me so we only saw each other on the weekends at rodeos. There were a couple of times I skipped school and drove down to see him. Looking back now, I see how wrong my priorities were and how blind I was to the truth. In fact, I was a very sick young girl on the inside and things were about to get a whole lot worse for me.

The relationship had become very controlling and I didn't even realize it. It wasn't that he would say mean things, but he got very jealous and that turned into manipulation and control through what seemed to be his love for me. Neither one of us knew any better. We tried to plan ways so we could see each other. We did anything we could to spend more time together. Entering the same rodeos was usually how we got around it. Before too long though, that wasn't enough. We wanted more of each other's time. We did the only thing we knew would give us more time together, and that was to have a baby.

This would be a great "plan." Our parents wouldn't be able to separate us. We would have a great excuse to have to be together. We would have our own family, our own space and the baby would bring us closer together! I knew when we talked about this "plan" that it was crazy. I also thought the plan would not actually happen. I was so far away from reality that I actually said "yes" to the plan and then believed this wouldn't happen to me!

Looking back now, I wonder how I could be so incredibly naïve? My best friend was pregnant and due in August. Her sister was due at any moment. They were both still in high school. How could I think this couldn't happen to me or think that somehow this was a good idea? I witnessed my best friend's tears, heartache, confusion, and the very hard decisions she had to make when she found out she was pregnant. Was I just not facing reality at all? Was I so broken that I didn't care? Had I lost my self-worth? Did I think this "plan" would give it back to me? Thinking back on all these things, I believe it was all the above. I was truly oblivious and truly had no self-worth.

This will all come as a complete shock to many who knew me in high school. I made good grades. I was great at sports. I had plenty of friends. I could enjoy myself and my time at places, parties and events. But on the inside, I did not have self-worth, morals, or standards. Nor did I believe that I was a girl that could hold out until she found the perfect guy. I just did not have that control. I jumped at almost any semi-cute guy that even remotely shared some of my same interests.

Stupid or not, Tony and I followed through with our plan. I got pregnant the summer before my senior year.

I took a pregnancy test at a gas station in Pittsburg, Texas on my way to my high school credit classes at Northeast Texas Community College in Mount Pleasant, Texas. It read positive almost immediately. There was no doubt in my mind. I was pregnant. The next few weeks are kind of a blur for me. At some point I know I told my best friend I was pregnant. I don't even remember telling her.

I mentioned earlier that I was writing a paper on abortion and lots of facts were presented to me. I was in control of that research. I read many truths about what an abortion is and what it entails. I read about the powerful devices and vacuums. I read how many women have an abortion each year and even argued my case on why abortion was wrong. But somewhere in my research, there was a gap. Some things were left out about the truth about abortion. If I read it, then once again, I was just blind and oblivious.

What I never read was that abortion doesn't just kill a baby, it kills the mother too. Nothing could have prepared me for the next ten years of hidden grief. I was facing a decade of loneliness, heartache, control, anger, guilt, and shame.

Chapter 3:

The Choice

When I first told my mom I was pregnant one hot summer day in late July, I had every intention of having a sweet, beautiful baby. We were sitting outside our horse trailer in Shawnee, Oklahoma at a high school rodeo. We were there for a solid week.

It was a very humbling experience to tell her. I was very nervous and didn't know how I was going to say it. It just came out, I couldn't hold it in any longer. Tony was sitting right there when I told her. I simply said, "Mom, I'm pregnant." I remember silence. I don't remember her saying anything back to me.

Next, we told his dad. I don't remember telling him at all. Maybe Tony told him without me there.

Over the next month, selfishness began to rise in me. I started thinking about all the things I would miss out on, volleyball games I wouldn't be able to play and what my friends would think about me. I thought about their lives and how they were going to blossom. They were going to enter into a whole new life, become educated, and meet new and interesting people, while I'm at the house being forgotten.

I thought about how I would be living off mom's paycheck too. I even called Tony's mom, who lived in California. We talked to her about moving in with her if Tony's dad wouldn't support us. She was understanding because she gave birth to

Tony when she was very young. She was about to be a grandmother and was still in her 30's! She was supportive but informed us that if we needed financial help, she would not be giving it.

That was quite a turn of the tables for me. In the back of my mind, I knew I would never be able to move to California and away from my family, anyway. Things seemed to be snowballing. I was ashamed at the choice I had made. I was embarrassed to be a teenage mother, insecure about the future, and selfish. I had to make a choice.

I don't know who mentioned it or how abortion even came up. I really don't even remember discussing it with anyone. What I do remember was flying home from my brother's Little League World Series baseball game that summer. We were in Minnesota for him to play.

There is no telling what my dad and brother thought about me going home. I don't even know what excuse I gave them. I most likely gave the excuse of, "I miss my boyfriend." And they probably accepted it without asking any more questions. What a lame excuse for a seventeen-year-old! They had to have known something weird was going on, but they never said anything.

I flew home with the coach's wife and their little boy. He cried the entire flight home. I cried invisible tears, concealed my heart and kept secret what was being orchestrated.

Over the next few days, plans began to unfold. Tony's dad made a few calls and I made a pre--appointment with Planned Parenthood. This pre-appointment was required since I was underage. When we walked in through those double glass doors of the affiliate building to Planned Parenthood and up to the check-in desk, things became a lot different. I anxiously began trying to hurry things up. The lady at the counter told me I either had to have them call my parents for consent or get a judge to push this through.

It doesn't make sense to me now but for some reason I didn't want them calling my mom. I remember feeling the shame even though she already knew. I remember making phone calls while I was in that office, and getting so frustrated with everyone I talked to. The lady behind the desk was looking at me like I was morbid. I'm pretty sure I even threw my hands down and groaned loudly after I got off the phone. Some way or another the appointment was made, and I did not go through a judge. They must have spoken to my mom and gotten the authorization to make the appointment. They could have even called Tony's dad. I was so manipulative at the time that I probably lied to them.

On the day of my appointment I walked the walk of death into Planned Parenthood ready to get rid of my problem. I walked up the stairs, into the waiting room, paid my money, and laid down on an ultrasound table. The nurse that did the ultrasound was a very tall lady. All of her emotions were off. This was a place of death and mortality. Why does everyone seem to be okay? They were so cold and she was no exception.

The emotions in that place are very hard to explain. Inside you're screaming and wanting out, ready to be done and wishing that this would all just go away. But the people there are opposite of what you're feeling or needing. They're just as secretive as you are and entirely focused on the *job*. They turn a blind eye. They don't see *you*.

As she performed the ultrasound, the picture screen was behind me and I could faintly see it out of the corner of my eye. I tried with everything in me not to look at it or even notice it. I tried to block it out. I tried not to see what I saw. I tried to focus on what I was there to do, but I couldn't. I saw my baby. I saw the little peanut-sized baby with hands, a face, little bitty feet. Everything that was there told me that this was a baby. This was a life. My own flesh and blood. This was a child.

The next words she spoke will never be erased from my memory: "8-6." Eight weeks and six days pregnant. That's how old my baby was, living inside me. That still didn't stop me. Seeing that image on the screen, knowing exactly how old the baby was, seeing that baby was a part of me, still wasn't something I could accept.

The nurse walked me down a hallway into another room. The procedure room. They offered me a choice of drugs and explained to me that I could take the ibuprofen drug, or I could also take a drug that would make me drowsy and somewhat sedated. I chose the combination of the two. I wanted anything that would numb the pain I was feeling. I wanted to be as separated from this as I possibly could be.

The doctor came in. I don't remember seeing him or saying anything. He asked a nurse a few questions and again I heard "8-6". A loud vacuum came on and then I felt an excruciating pain in my abdomen area. I screamed and a nurse who was holding my hand told me to be quiet because they didn't want other girls outside in the halls to hear me. They might change their minds.

There was no mercy, no compassion. Just get in, get done, get out. I remember the pain seemed to last forever. I remember holding the nurse's hand but at the same time hating that I needed someone there to hold it. She was only holding my hand because of the physical pain I was feeling. She didn't actually care for me. She didn't care about my emotional pain at all. In reality, she was probably just as numb as I was to her emotions and feelings.

How could you practice that job day in and day out without becoming hardened to the reality of human life? I suppose in some twisted way they believe they're doing women a "service" by allowing this "choice." They believe they're helping these women by allowing them a chance to have a future. They believe the lie that children can be a hindrance to young women who still want to go to college and have a career, or for the couple who "can't afford a child right now." For the women who have a far different life style than mine, like drugs, homelessness, prostitution, etcetera and get pregnant, the lie gets even deeper. They say these women are better off getting an abortion because that baby just doesn't have a chance.

These are all lies. Every child is created in God's image and the child isn't accidentally placed in the womb because of a one-night stand or a one-time choice. I am not saying sex anytime anywhere is okay but I am saying God places every child in the womb strategically. Look at Jesus – He was placed in a virgin's womb at exactly the right time and was called to a purpose for the Kingdom of God. Every child holds that same gift. You hold that same gift according to God's will for your life.

Somewhere in our logical thinking, we begin to esteem success and money over a child and the value that God puts on a human life. We forget the joy that children bring, the laughter they create, and the blessing that God says they are. Children are a blessing to our heritage.

Eventually, the sound of the life-sucking vacuum turned off. The pain subsided, and everyone left the room. A few minutes later, a nurse walked back in the room to check on me and helped me to a recovery room. After about 30 minutes, from what I can recall, I was sent home with a brown paper bag stuffed with papers and two months' worth of birth control. I met my boyfriend in the waiting room and we walked to the truck. There I was. It was done. It was over. What more was there to worry about?

Or was there?

Driving away I felt so empty, so alone, so heartbroken and shameful. The guilt was beginning to pile on already. Afterwards, it was only Tony and me. We pulled into a grocery store not far down the road, and I talked to my mom on the phone before we went in. The anger had already begun. Nobody knew what to say. Nobody really knew how to feel. I had made a choice. It was supposed to be the right choice, so why did it feel so wrong? The only words I remember from that phone conversation were my mother's words as, in a shaky and sorrowful voice she said, "I feel like I should be there for you."

Those words hit me hard. She was just as confused as I was. In a way, yes, I wanted her there with me to comfort and console me, to hold me and hug me and tell me everything was going to be okay. But in another way, I didn't want to show my weakness, my hurt, or my pain. It was easier to seek the things I needed from my mom in my boyfriend, but it just didn't compare to the love of a parent. I was too ashamed to talk to my mom about it. I told myself everything would be fine.

Walking into that grocery store, everything felt so wrong. Here I was planning my next meal! Tony was awkwardly trying to make me feel better and picking out "fancy" foods as if there was some kind of celebration taking place. He wasn't celebrating what we had done – he was just trying to make me feel better. Nothing could make me feel better at that moment. All I could do was put on a mask and pretend like everything was okay. I would pick up right where I left off. I would finish high school, play volleyball, and get ready for college.

Life would go on.

Chapter 4:

Festering Wounds

For the first couple of months, things didn't seem so bad. I would think about the abortion often but as soon as it came to my mind, I stuffed it out. That worked for a while but eventually, I became very tormented. Once everyone was settled in for bed for the night and I was all alone in my bedroom, thoughts began to consume me. To be honest, these thoughts and visions weren't even of my abortion. They were of my doctor's visit a few weeks after the abortion. I went to see a gynecologist so I could get on birth control. My two-month supply was running out. I remember sitting in the doctor's office the day of my first OB-GYN appointment thinking, I wouldn't be here had I not had an abortion. Or, at least, I wouldn't be here under these circumstances. I went to my best friend's doctor. She loved him and he had delivered her beautiful baby boy just months earlier.

I sat down in the waiting room filling out paperwork and medical history. One of the questions asked if I ever had an abortion. Well, that was the only reason I was there! I was honest this first time and checked "Yes", but I never marked that I had an abortion ever again.

Soon I was called back to see the doctor. As I waited in the exam room wearing nothing but a gown, my heart was racing 100 miles per hour. I heard the door open and was immediately drenched with sweat. The next thing I heard would feed my anger for years to come. It would resound in my mind over and over. It fed the control that I always felt I needed to maintain after this day. The doctor walked in and said, "Did your mom make you come today?"

That was the absolute worst thing that could have been said to a hurting, nervous, lonely, angry, seventeen-year-old. It might not make sense to anyone else, but it hit a nerve in me that began throbbing with pain. There was no compassion, I was just another patient to him.

I answered him with a simple, "No."

We talked for just a moment. I don't really remember what was said but I believe we talked about why I was getting on birth control, and he knew at this point that I had had an abortion. As I laid back on the exam table, I had no idea what was about to happen. Pap smears and pelvic exams were just words to me. I knew my vagina was going to be looked at and tested. I knew there were going to be instruments used to "scrape" my cervix, but I did not know what it involved entirely.

As the doctor began the exam, he used instruments that touched me in areas that I was unaware would be touched. He felt every area of my breasts and touched every place on my body that was mine. I felt completely vulnerable and low. I felt disgusting and dirty. I felt completely exposed and downright degraded. Every part of my body that was supposed to be mine and not for a complete stranger to touch and feel, especially in this way, left me feeling totally dismayed. Then, when he inserted his very own hands into my vagina I was completely taken aback. I was shocked and mortified. I wasn't prepared for this exam, even after having sexual relations and an abortion. I was petrified, which sent me spiraling into an all-time low.

Maybe because I was so doped up during the abortion, the exams that happened there didn't bother me so badly. This time I was completely sober-minded and had nothing in my system. There was nothing to dull the moment, and no mask to hide behind. Whatever it was, this day would mark the day that I could not live with myself at night. This would mark the beginning of years of torture, heartache, guilt, shame, and self-hatred.

After the exam was over, he talked to me for a little bit longer. I wanted him to say something that would take all of this away. I wanted him to tell me everything would be okay and I could move on. As I sat there, still in my gown, I don't know what all I said but I remember he asked me if I'd had thoughts of suicide. I just shook my head no. I wasn't suicidal, but I was severely depressed and ashamed.

What strikes me now, looking back, is that doctor knew the tale-tale signs of abortion. They are PTSD-like symptoms. Depression, anger, control, flashbacks, suicide, eating disorders, excessive crying, drinking, drugs, etcetera. He did not offer me any help whatsoever. The lack of compassion fed my anger even more.

After leaving that appointment, I was marked for torment. The physical sensations caused real emotional wounds that would last more than a decade. The enemy remembered me that day. The wounds that had been festering inside me became infected and agitated. Emotionally I was bleeding, and I left a trail everywhere I stepped. No matter what path I took, no matter what I did, the enemy had found my blood trail and he was following me every step of the way.

Chapter 5:

Night Terrors

Sleepless nights became a friend of mine. Two o'clock, even three o'clock in the morning would come before I could fall asleep. Then I'd wake up at 6:30 a.m. to get to school. It's a wonder how I even passed my classes.

I was terrified of nights. I became anxious and fearful. I would talk on the phone and cry to Tony every night about what I was feeling and how I wanted things to go away. I would cry, scream, and lash out and yet all the while, my family had no idea this was happening. I remember one night I was on the phone with him and I was so angry that I began groaning at him in frustration and screaming on the phone. The next day my mom said, laughingly, "One of you (my brother's room was next to mine) must have been talking in your sleep last night. I kept hearing this groaning noise over and over. It woke me up from my sleep."

She had no idea what I was going through. The darkness in my mind had become so deep that I had to sleep with the light on in the bathroom next to my room. I had to fall asleep to the sound of the television so my mind wouldn't drift into torment and terror of the guilt and shame I felt.

The physical feelings were the worst. I was not usually taken back to the day of the abortion as much as I was the day in the gynecologist's exam room. The physical feeling of the exam and the fondling of the doctor's hands were all that I could think about. I would do anything I could to try and take my mind and body away from that feeling. I had flashbacks, hearing over and over the words of all the doctors and nurses, and I couldn't make them stop. These episodes usually left me curled up in the fetal position with my hands between my legs trying to cover up as I was assaulted with the physical sensations. I would cry, and cry, and cry. The enemy tortured me with that exam.

I was very much like a victim of molestation, and I experienced many of the same symptoms. I felt dirty and unworthy. I couldn't tell anyone what happened to me because I was too ashamed. I wanted desperately to stop the whispers and the humiliation that had imprisoned me in my own body and mind.

Any time conversation was brought up about abortion or the gynecologist, I had to walk away. I couldn't handle it. I couldn't listen to commercials, news reports, or anything else that mentioned those two words. I changed the channel and did everything I could to run from it. The words caused me too much pain and anger.

Once I was prescribed birth control, I tried taking the pill every morning. Just to look at the package of pills served as a bitter reminder of what I had done. Anger would rise up in me first thing in the morning before heading off to school. I was miserable. I was so mad about the birth control and so mad at doctors and nurses for saying I "had to have this exam." I didn't understand why I couldn't refuse the exam and know that I was taking a risk of having something wrong with me. The risk of the mental attacks was far worse than something being physically wrong with me. Why couldn't I just take the pill at my own risk and sign a waiver saying I didn't care if something was wrong with me? We allow abortions and the killing of babies but there's no opt-out waiver for a woman to sign saying she understands the health risk of taking a pill?

One day I got so mad that I called the doctor's office and talked to a nurse. I must have wanted to change my prescription or wanted to do something different. I knew that the birth control pills were making my anger much worse, so I had an excuse to call and I didn't care how I treated people at this point. Hurt people hurt people. By the end of the conversation, I made up my mind that I wasn't even going to take the birth control pills and I told that nurse how I felt. She was a little bit confused but also treated me like I was stupid. I *was* being stupid but there was so much more going on with me. That was my mindset.

Sometimes we simply need to ask, "What's really going on here?" If someone would have just talked to me and shown me love I wouldn't have been so mad. Sometimes we just need to say, "What happened? I'm here to listen."

I hated myself. I hated what I had done. Sometimes I drifted off into daydreams about how far along I would be. The baby would have been due in February – we would have shared the same birth month. I wondered if it would have been a boy or a girl? I imagined a boy and what I would have named him.

Sometimes I would drift off into thinking about really odd things like what I wore that day, or the steps I took that led up to the abortion. In my mind, I could change the outcome. I would stand up to the doctors and nurses and tell them how much I hated them and that I was not going through with this! I would think, and think, and think, but nothing ever changed.

This pattern of torment and mental anguish lasted many years.

I graduated high school that following May and moved into my college dorm room in August of 2005. I received a volleyball scholarship as well as a rodeo scholarship to Hill College in Hillsboro, Texas. As a volleyball player, I moved in early because I had to be there before the semester started. But because I was also on the rodeo team, I lived in the rodeo dorm, which was a completely different building from the volleyball team. There was absolutely no one in this building besides me and maybe a dorm mom. I didn't have a television and this was before smart phones, so the first night was one of the most haunting and fearful nights of my entire life. I wanted out. I wanted friends. I wanted to be held, hugged, and I hated being so alone. Loneliness and fear were two of my greatest companions.

During those few weeks before anyone moved into the dorms, I kept myself as busy as possible. As soon as volleyball practice was over, I would head to the barn and saddle my horses and ride. There was only so much I could do to keep myself from courting loneliness and fear. When the day slowed down, here they came. They did everything they could to slip their way into my thoughts, mind, and emotions.

Once the semester started, things got a little easier. My roommate brought a television and there always seemed to be someone around to help occupy any downtime. I filled my extra time with books, volleyball, horses, friends, and my boyfriend. Tony and I were still dating and agreed to go to college together. I guess I really went there because that's where he wanted to go. I got a partial volleyball scholarship and that's all I wanted.

Before too long, things got to be too much between he and I. We were living together during the spring semester, and we fought and bickered a lot. I had quit the volleyball team by this point. He was very jealous and didn't have the ambition or life goals that I wanted in someone.

When I broke up with him, we were in front of the Hill College library, standing between two parked cars and he was sobbing. Through tears, he told me he thought about the baby often and he wanted to be able to look at our baby and see me. He looked down and held his arms out as if he were holding a child in his arms and said that the reason he wanted to have the baby in the first place was to be able to have something to remember me by if I ever left him.

I felt deeply sorry for him. I hated he was feeling this way because of me. When your feelings for someone have changed and you can't make those old feelings ignite, it only makes the break-up process more painful the longer the relationship lingers. It's more painful for the one who still wants the relationship but only more repulsive for the one leaving.

Truth be told, I had a new attraction. He was a bareback rider at Hill and I liked his joyful personality. Everyone seemed to like him, and he had ambition. So, after a year-and-a-half-long relationship during the darkest hours of my life, I cut ties with the old and in came the new. Just like every other relationship before this one. I moved from one to the next and I justified my actions because they were all "long-term" relationships. This new one was a good excuse to move on from my past. Or, at least I was trying to.

Chapter 6:

Promiscuous Girl

The summer of 2006 was a lot of fun. The new guy, Jack, qualified for the College National Finals Rodeo in Casper, Wyoming in the bareback riding. I was not going to miss watching him ride! Plus, I wanted to travel and have fun. So, another girl (whose boyfriend also qualified for the CNFR) and I packed up my little yellow Volkswagen Beetle and drove to Wyoming.

After a speeding ticket and a broken windshield along the way, we made it safe and sound. It was honestly not the greatest ride of my life and I was very angry over the broken windshield and ticket. The friend that rode with me had an argument with her mom on the phone. She slammed her phone down on the dash and it bounced up and shattered the entire windshield like a spiderweb! I didn't say a word to her as she kept repeating "I'm sorry, I'm sorry!"

All of those emotions melted away though when I saw Jack step out of his old maroon big-body Cadillac. I remember running towards him and jumping into his arms. He held me in his arms while his mom, who was quite the character, stood to the side smiling and laughing. She had not met me yet but was delighted to see him so happy. I was happy as well, and never thought I would want anything more.

When the summer ended, we both headed back to Hill College to finish out our associate degrees. We both needed another year of school at Hill, so we decided to get a house together. That suited me just fine. The nights were still haunting for me and this would soothe those demons that liked to torment me when I was alone. Jack knew someone that had rental houses in the area and, sure enough, we found a little house with a few extra bedrooms in case family members wanted to come down and visit.

Although my "new life" had begun, it didn't take long for the fresh to wear off. About two-and-a-half years into the relationship, I got bored. We were now in Huntsville, Texas at Sam Houston State University. Both of us were still rodeoing. We were still living together, and things got very difficult. There was so much striving. Money was always an issue and he expected me to pay my way as if I was his roommate. I guess I really was. We weren't married, and I was still receiving money from my parents. Essentially, we were just playing house.

I was working at a restaurant that had an atmosphere like Hooter's bar. It was a sports bar and grill called "Tops and Bottoms." You can imagine. We wore tiny spandex volleyball shorts and black-and-white referee tank tops. One of the girls that rodeoed with me at Hill also transferred to Sam Houston. We stayed good friends and got the job together. We figured the tips would be great money while finishing school.

During this time, I met another guy named Cory. Cory was tall and handsome, and I was very attracted to him. Jack was a smaller guy and I didn't have much of a physical attraction to him anymore. I still loved him, but I was bored with our relationship. I wanted some excitement and something new again!

I don't remember where I met Cory but one night I told Jack I was going to stay the night with a girlfriend from the bar where I worked. I did leave with her and we rode in her car, but we didn't stay at her house. We stayed at Cory's house. I barely knew this guy and she had no idea who he was or who his friends were. He had a few friends staying at the house that night. She slept on the couch with one of them (who knew Jack fairly well) and I stayed in Cory's bed. It was my first one-night stand. Of course, I didn't want it to be a one-night thing, I wanted it to be more. I was one of those girls who blew up your phone. I was one of those girls that if I liked you I wasn't going to leave easily. I was one of those girls that needed to know someone liked her to be content. I didn't care much if girls liked me or not, I just needed to know someone was attracted to me and cared about me intimately.

The next morning, my friend and I got our things together and left. As we were driving home we passed Jack in his car on the way to school. He never knew it was me and he never knew what happened. He really believed I stayed the night with a friend from work and that I was honest and sincere with him. The guy at Cory's house never told Jack what happened, but my guilt and shame started to stack up.

I couldn't take much more. I decided to break up with Jack and move out. I had talked myself into being able to live on my own and do the roommate thing. I could do it! We ended up breaking up and he even helped me move into my new place. He was not happy with it and we remained "friends." I claimed that I wanted to remain friends with him but that never really worked out. After living together and having a life together you can't just become friends. I don't think we were split up for more than a month. I just couldn't stand being alone and he really did care for me. We got back together and we moved back in with each other.

I ended up cheating on him with someone else; same story pretty much. I went out with a girlfriend and met someone, stayed the night with him, slept with him, then he wanted nothing to do with me even though I wanted something to do with him.

There were some girl friends that lived close to me and we talked a lot. We all lived on the same property and we were all on the Sam Houston Rodeo team. I bragged to them that I had slept with two guys and Jack didn't know about it. We were talking on their front porch about our one night stands as if we were trying to one-up each other or say, "Look what I've done." Truth be told, I was just jealous of their single lives and their contentment to stay single; or at least, they portrayed that they were content being single. They could definitely spend their nights alone with no problem, which was something I still couldn't do.

I don't know how everything went down but one of the girls spilled the news to Jack that I had cheated on him and not with just one person. It was multiple guys at different times and he had no idea about them. He moved out and was very disappointed in me. He was heartbroken and even still wanted to try and work things out, but I knew things were not going to work out for us. I hated myself for what I had done to him.

I was so hard-hearted at this point I couldn't even grasp the heartache I caused him. I know now that betrayal by someone you love is among the worst pain anyone can inflict. He trusted me, and I betrayed him. I cut him deep. At the time, I could not see his hurt. I could not understand what I had truly done to him.

Finding Freedom

    Following the 2011 spring semester, I moved back home with my mom. I had my Bachelor's degree from Sam Houston State University in Interdisciplinary Studies and had a few graduate courses under my belt. This time, I was truly committed to staying at home and being content. Jack went back home to South Dakota. I enrolled in graduate classes at the University of Texas at Tyler in Tyler, Texas, and began riding horses for income. Although Jack and I were separated, we were still in a relationship. Now that we were done with college it seemed possible that we might even get married.

Chapter 7:

A Shift

While I was living at home with my mom, I began going to church and giving my tithe. I attended the Methodist church that we had always attended when I was growing up. My grandmother really liked the new pastor and she talked highly of him. Almost every Sunday I attended church with my grandmother and I was enjoying it. It made me feel good, but I never truly got anything out of it.

I went in once to talk to the pastor. I had a few questions for him. I was taking graduate courses to become a counselor. I really liked learning things about the mind and how it worked. In one of my classes, there were actually Christian counseling theories and methods we learned about. That really intrigued me. I asked the pastor of the church at that time if they ever did anything like that. I was feeling things out, trying to find my way and keep my options open. It was not anything I was trying to jump into without having experience and a degree. I was planning for the future, and wanted to understand my options for future plans.

One of his responses to me was, "You need to get your schooling done first."

"WELL DUH!" I thought to myself. "What does he think I'm trying to do?" He seriously thought I was trying to start counseling sessions by having this meeting with him. That happened to me numerous times.

While I was taking these counseling classes, my stepdad was struggling with opioid addiction. He had been addicted to pain pills since my brother was born, at least 20 years, and had even been to rehab. By this time, he was on methadone and was abusing that when he could. He found ways to get what he wanted, as any addict does. Things got really bad, so I went to one of my professors, hoping he could get us in touch with a good rehab and counseling facility. They were counselors in the region, so I thought they were going to have the answers I needed.

I talked to him in his office and he came to the same conclusion that the pastor did! He thought I was going to try and counsel my family myself! What was twisting my words so badly that they thought I was going to run the show that way? This same professor later told me my writing was like an elementary child's story and he couldn't understand it at all. I did not go back the next semester. I knew that was a lie, and I knew my paper wasn't the best, but to compare it to an elementary paper was pretty damaging. It was too much work anyway, and the only reason I was pursuing it was because Jack wanted me to.

I felt like I needed to prove something through this Master's degree. Jack always told me that a teaching degree was less than a degree; as if the work I did wasn't intelligent work. Maybe it wasn't, but teaching was what I wanted to do regardless of how smart the work was or how smart I was.

Living at home gave me freedom. I didn't have to pay rent and I was able to help my mom out here and there. My mom and stepdad had divorced during my junior year of college and finances were tight. I was able to at least have satellite TV hooked up for us and it made me feel good that I could assist financially in some way. She helped me tremendously during college, even after the divorce. They paid for almost everything. The money I made was usually just extra.

I began riding outside horses to make some money when I moved back home. I was riding a lot with a friend who lived close by. Her name was Robin. I grew up rodeoing with Robin and her family. They've always had nice horses. Her mom, Theresa, hauled with us when I was young. We went to all the amateur rodeos around East Texas together. She was also attending classes in Tyler so our schedules coincided. We had a great time training and riding together that semester. It was the spring of 2011, just before the drought hit Texas so badly that summer. One weekend, Theresa had tickets to a Baptist women's conference, and she was not able to attend. Since Robin was already going, she offered me Theresa's ticket. I accepted the offer and was happy to attend this event, called Feminar. I had never been to a women's weekend conference before, but I was really looking forward to it. After all, I was becoming very "religious." I wanted to know more about Jesus, and church had become a regular thing for me on Sundays. I was hungry to know more.

When that Friday night rolled around, we loaded in Robin's car and headed to the conference. I had no idea what I was about to experience, sitting there about eight rows back. The whole auditorium was full, about three balconies high. They had awesome praise and worship bands. It was a little awkward for me because I didn't know the words to the songs. Even though the lyrics were displayed on two huge big screens above me, I was embarrassed that I didn't know these Christian songs like everyone else did. I was very self-conscious about someone knowing I didn't know what I was singing, I swayed back and forth to the music and tried not looking up at the big screen to read the lyrics. It was like I thought I was "supposed" to know.

As praise and worship came to an end and we all took our seats, the two big screens, one on my right and one on my left, lit up with a face and a story began to unfold. As the woman shared her testimony, I couldn't believe what I was hearing. All I wanted to do was cover my ears and run out of that auditorium. I couldn't imagine someone could be talking about what she was talking about!

How could someone come right out and say, "I've had an abortion?" How could she even say that word? Why is she so calm about sharing that? All I can remember is wanting to crawl under my seat. I wanted to cringe at every word she said. I knew in reality that nobody knew I had had an abortion but inside of me I felt like everyone was looking at me! I sensed everybody knew my secret. I felt like there was no way I could ever talk about my abortion like this. It was a very uncomfortable experience for me.

Finally, the story came to an end and the seminar moved on. Later on that night during a brief break, I walked out into the foyer where different ministries had their tables set up. In one corner, there was a table for Christ Centered Abortion Recovery and Education, C.A.R.E.

I approached the table but walked by from a distance, just close enough to observe their materials. There were books and resources sitting out but I couldn't bring myself to walk up to that table. I walked past it three or four times trying to catch a glimpse of the books and information. I caught the title of a book and quickly wrote it down in my notes on my phone. I may have even written some other titles down, but I remember them being saved in my phone for a long time. I never actually ordered them or read them, though. I couldn't bring myself to face my past.

When I got home that night, I went through the goodie bags that had been handed out at the door as we arrived. I knew there were brochures in there from C.A.R.E. I began pulling things out of the bag until I came to one postcard that listed the side effects of abortion that every woman might experience. I was amazed at what I read. The symptoms ranged from flashbacks to eating disorders. Nightmares, guilt, regret, drugs, alcohol, excessive crying, anger, suicidal thoughts, emptiness, anxiety and more. Just like with anything else, each person's experience and emotional state will be personal and unique to them.

So many of the symptoms on the card were what I experienced. As I read them, all of a sudden I felt like I was not alone. Something inside me said I wasn't crazy, and that I wasn't experiencing these emotions for no reason. I couldn't believe I wasn't the only one feeling this way. It was such a relief and I wanted to hear more.

I went back to Feminar the next day with Robin. I wanted more of what they were pouring out. I wanted to know more and experience more. There were many speakers over the two-day conference but it was Janet White who had the biggest impact on me. I couldn't help but soak in everything she said. It was like every word that came out of her mouth that day was replacing a lie that I had believed all my life.

Her message was on family values. She shared about her children but most of all she shared about her marriage. She spoke simply and modeled in words what a healthy marriage looked like. In all of my life, a healthy, strong marriage had never been modeled for me. All she did was talk about how much she loved her husband. She joked about little things they would do for each other and how each one gave a little and took a little from time to time. She spoke about the strength of their marriage and how much they adored each other. She told stories about how mad he could make her, and then turned it around by sharing how God was able to change her heart through their disagreement. It was then that I realized how twisted my thinking about men had been growing up. Here I was 24 years old and I wasn't anywhere near being ready to have a marriage like I had always wanted and longed for.

I always thought a man wanted a girl who would do what they wanted. I always thought a man wanted "one thing." I always thought that if I could flaunt myself just right I could get and keep a guy much easier. I always thought if I acted "tough" or showed off in front of them I could get them. I even thought that I really could get any guy I wanted and that the other guys were jealous if they couldn't have me! I actually thought that way.

After listening to Janet speak that night I realized that men really do want one woman in their life. They need to know they are needed. A woman to a man is like the wind beneath his wings. If the husband doesn't have the wind he cannot go higher. A woman's role in a man's life is to be their encourager, their companion. We are there to let them know they are doing a great job.

"22Wives, submit to your own husbands, as to the Lord. 23For the husband is head of the wife, as also Christ is head of the church; and He is the Savior of the body. 24Therefore, just as the church is subject to Christ, so let the wives be to their own husbands in everything. 25Husbands, love your wives, just as Christ also loved the church and gave Himself for her, 26that He might sanctify and cleanse her with the washing of water by the word, 27that He might present her to Himself a glorious church, not having spot or wrinkle or any such thing, but that she should be holy and without blemish. 28So husbands ought to love their own wives as their own bodies; he who loves his wife loves himself. 29For no one ever hated his own flesh, but nourishes and cherishes it, just as the Lord does the church. 30For we are members of His body, of His flesh and of His bones. 31'For this reason a man shall leave his father and mother and be joined to his wife, and the two shall become one flesh.' 32This is a great mystery, but I speak concerning Christ and the church. 33Nevertheless let each one of you in particular so love his own wife as himself, and let the wife see that she respects her husband." – Ephesians 5:22-33 New King James Version (NKJV)

The Bible says a man needs respect and reverence ("phobeo" in Greek, Strong's G5399) and a woman needs love ("agapao" in Greek, Strong's G25). There are multiple words used for the wife from submit to reverence. The Greek word "phobeo" is actually a word that can be translated "to fear."[6] It

---

[6] G5399 - phobeō - Strong's Greek Lexicon (KJV). Retrieved from *https://www.blueletterbible.org//lang/lexicon/lexicon.cfm?Strongs=g5399&t=kjv*

means that women are to fear our husbands the way we would fear the Lord. We stand in awe of Jesus and the Word tells us to stay in awe of our husbands. His place in the home is to be the decision-maker, the load-bearer, and the one who provides for the ones he loves. This place of authority carries with it a great responsibility!

The husband is to love his wife with agape love just like Jesus loves the Church, His Bride. According to Thayer's Greek Lexicon, the word "agapao" as used in verse 25 tells the husband that he is "to have a preference for, to wish well to, regard the welfare of"[7] his wife. The Americanized meaning of "submit" and "reverence" has taken on such a negative connotation that now we want to argue that these verses are "old school" and "nobody does that anymore." In turn, marriages have failed because the Church has failed to interpret these verses the correct way. The point Paul is trying to make through these verses is that the husband and the wife both have a role in representing Christ in their marriage as they lift each other up and encourage each other; the wife through being in awe of her husband and the husband through loving his wife with agape love.

Many times, we try to influence our husbands to show us love and when we try to show them love, we don't understand why they don't accept it like we would. When you show your husband respect, you show him that you are yielded to him the way you would Jesus, and he will naturally show you love back. It is about showing him the honor he deserves – not

---

[7] G25 - agapaō - Strong's Greek Lexicon (KJV). Retrieved from
https://www.blueletterbible.org//lang/lexicon/lexicon.cfm?Strongs=g25&t=kjv

because of what he has done but because of who God made him to be and the potential he has.

The following year I attended Feminar again, and again, I heard another abortion testimony. This one was a testimony of God's healing in her life after she had not just one, but two abortions! That blew me away. How could someone go back to such a traitorous place? It didn't make sense to me, but now I know there are women who have had multiple abortions for many different reasons. Most of the time, nobody knows except one or two other people. It is a secret and they don't want anyone to find out about the choice they are making. It is a wicked cycle, but God's grace and forgiveness surpasses all of it!

That first year of Feminar would prepare me for something I was never expecting. God had His hand on every detail of my life and at that time, I didn't even know Him. He loves us so much that even in our darkness He will guide us and prepare us for what is to come.

Chapter 8:

Marriage & Family

A few months after attending my first Feminar, I met my future husband. I know now that God orchestrated Theresa not being able to go to Feminar that year. He was preparing me for a great marriage and a godly life. He had the perfect plan in mind and the perfect man prepared for me.

He was the full package. I met Galen at a garage sale I was having after moving home from college. He came over with my cousin and bought a blue recliner from me. We cooked out at the house that night and he joined us. It was Memorial weekend in late May and there was a lot going on. We ended up hanging out all weekend. He was fun and he loved to dance. That was always something I desired in my future husband. He had beautiful lips, he was tall with dark hair and dark features, his hands were working man's hands, and we were able to laugh together. The next day (Sunday), we went to Shreveport for the Mudbug Madness festival and stayed all day. It was HOT, but we danced and ate crawfish until we couldn't eat anymore. On Memorial Day Monday, we went to the lake and had a blast once again. I was 24 years old, and he was 21.

I really liked him but there was one problem: I still had a boyfriend in South Dakota. I had to break up with him, and I knew it wasn't going to be easy. After five years, you can't just call it quits very easily. I was also going to have to do it over the phone because he was so far away. It was not the best way to break up with someone but I had to because I did not want my new relationship to look anything like the ones I had in the past. This was a new beginning for me and I was going to make it count.

The day that Jack came down to get his things, Galen was building fence. He knew Jack would be at my house and he was not happy about it. He knew it had to happen but it just didn't sit right with him. I remember him being very agitated. I even remember my mom getting on to me! When I told her Galen was upset about it, she told me I was wrong for being at the house while Jack was there! It shocked me because my mom has never scolded me like that. I didn't see it that way, but I understood after she pointed it out. However, at that point, it was too late, and Jack had gotten his things out. It was very awkward to say the least. He wanted me back and I was completely moved on and committed to this new relationship. He even had an engagement ring made for me. I saw it hanging from the gear shift in his truck. I know he put it there intending for me to see it, but it didn't change my mind one bit. I just looked away. Material things mean nothing without true feelings. I was over him and happy to be with Galen. He was so much healthier for me. We were a fit. It was wonderful.

Although my mind had changed on how to treat a man and I learned how their minds work in a relationship, I still didn't see anything wrong with staying at Galen's house with him. I still didn't have the power to stay by myself at night when I wanted to be with him so badly. I held off on calling Galen all the time and I tried my best to let him call me. I didn't give in to that crazy, overbearing, give-him-no-space kind of girl. That was a big step for me! He might say different, but I didn't scare him away.

It was a summer of love, no doubt! We went to South Padre Island about two months after we met and he told me he loved me one warm, windy night while we walked the sandy beaches. It was so perfect and it happened without a plan. He is not a romantic type by any means but he can when he has to. He was romantic enough to reel me in and catch me. I'm not big on a lot of romance either, so it works great for us!

He proposed to me that following June 2012, I took a new teaching job that following August, and we were married a year and four months after we met, on October 6, 2012. We found out we were pregnant the day we got back from our honeymoon (I was pregnant before we got married, actually), and eight months later Cole Thomas Hutton was born into this world. I was so excited to be a mom. I knew it was going to be the best thing that could happen to us! I wanted a baby and was ready to start a family with Galen. I knew he was going to be a great daddy.

Finding out I was pregnant was very emotional for me. The reality of what I was going to have to go through – and I don't mean the physical pain of childbirth – was a little overwhelming. After much thought, I decided that I was not going to use a doctor for this delivery. Thank goodness, Galen's mom used a midwife and even worked alongside a midwife after she had children. She told me of the many midwives in the area and shared her personal story of having a home birth. I chose the midwife she had worked so closely with and recommended.

At our first appointment, I was overwhelmed with the thought that they might tell me I "must" have a pap smear and pelvic exam. I couldn't hold back the tears. I couldn't let go of the awful emotions and the idea of having to do that again.

Thank goodness, which was the reason I chose a midwife, they told me that would not be a problem at all and I could waive the exam and deliver this baby without having to go through any of that. I waived every exam I could.

Now, I know some people will read this and think that I did not choose what was best for my child. In the medical field, doctors must make decisions when the "risk outweighs the benefit" and vice versa. I decided to decline these exams because the stress and anxiety would have caused more harm to my baby and me than going through something that would tell me what I already knew. I was fine. To each is their own decision, especially when it comes to delivering and raising our children. It took me many years to come to that conclusion. Nobody is going to do it your way – each one is going to do it his or her way. Perfectly acceptable in a world that tells us to be unique and be yourself. Your way is the best way for you.

I had an amazing delivery at the birthing center and couldn't have asked for a better husband and coach to stand by my side. During the early stages of labor, we ended up walking the streets of Tyler to try and speed up my labor. Looking back now, it's funny, but at the time I did not care. I was ready to birth this baby! As we walked during the early morning hours, a labor pain hit me right as we passed in front of a lady's house. She was sitting on her front porch as I crouched down and held onto Galen. There was a small highway in front of us and a car came by. Galen was trying to get me to stand up and the lady wanted to call the hospital. She didn't know what to think and Galen was worried about the people driving by! I didn't care, though. It was time for this delivery and I was doing everything I could.

After twenty-one hours of labor, Cole arrived. I was exhausted! When they put him in my arms all I remember saying, over and over again, was "my baby, my baby, my baby!" We were finally proud parents of a beautiful baby boy and he had my features. Blonde hair, light skin, and blue eyes. He was just perfect.

We took him home and settled in. Family came over the next day and all that little angel could do was sleep, sleep, sleep. Our little 600 square foot house was packed with loved ones that Sunday afternoon. I couldn't help but think how easy this was going to be.

Wow, was I wrong!

I so wanted to nurse Cole, but he wouldn't take to nursing and he cried and cried. I didn't want to give him a bottle and I felt like a failure of a mom for not being able to nurse him like I wanted to. I thought nursing would just happen, I thought it would be easy. This was harder than childbirth and way more emotional! I felt like giving him a bottle was like giving him poison. I just did. I don't know why I felt that way but I hated that bottles and formula had to be an option. I tried for a while but about four to six weeks after he was born I gave up. He didn't want to latch on and I didn't want to pump. I wanted to keep my social life a little too much and didn't realize that I was going to have to lay all of that down to nurse him the way I wanted to.

I remember many days lying in bed and letting him cry in the living room. I didn't know what to do for him and I couldn't get anything done. I couldn't get far enough away to drown out his crying, so it made my emotions even worse. I couldn't shower, I couldn't eat, I couldn't clean, and I especially didn't have any "me" time. It was early June and Galen loves to work, and summer means longer days. He didn't get home until seven or eight o' clock in the evening, and he didn't realize the stress I was going through.

I was depressed, no doubt about it. One time, my mother-in-law called to check on me and I couldn't even answer my phone. Cole was crying, I was lying in bed, and when the phone rang I just silenced it, rolled over, and bawled my eyes out. I wanted help, but I felt like I should know how to do this baby thing. I felt guilty for asking or even letting someone take him for a few hours, and especially overnight. In all honesty, to be transparent for anyone else who has experienced this, one day I called my mom and actually said "I hate my baby!"

What harsh words for a mother to say over her child, but that's exactly what I said. I couldn't take the crying and emotions anymore. My mom immediately took off work and came to my rescue. She came and picked Cole up, and he probably even stayed the night with her that night. There were many times she took him so I could recuperate. I was able to take a deep breath and go back to my precious baby, refreshed. I did not really hate my baby, I hated that I couldn't help him when he was crying. He did have a little bit of reflux but for the most part he was just a baby that was ready to move, go outside, and grow! He loved being outside and being held. That was something I had to learn the hard way. I had to lay down my selfish desires, my good housekeeping (if you can call it that), and my social time. He was a baby boy who was ready to be on the move, and he did just that! He crawled the day before he turned six months, walked at nine months and was busting through everything he could get his hands on at that point. He loved to be outside!

When the summer came to an end, I started back teaching while my mother-in-law watched Cole for me. When Cole was about four months old, we looked for a home to buy and we found a perfect house and piece of land. The property was only a mile-and-a-half down the road from our current location. We loved the area, so the property and house were picture-perfect for us. We decided to buy it!

Chapter 9:

Murder in the Parking Lot

At the same time we were looking to buy a house, my closest cousin, Cheyenne, was looking to move back to Gilmer with her son, Trenton. She had been roommates with the daughter of the woman from whom we were buying our house. She was able to rent our house and move in right away. Cheyenne was escaping a domestic violence situation with her son's father, James (not his real name) and had been informed by Child Protective Services that she had to leave or they would take her child from her.

We were excited to have her move in and I was excited to have her back in our lives. Galen had never really met her. Due to Cheyenne's dangerous relationship with James and his controlling nature, she wasn't allowed to visit or communicate with our family much. He didn't allow her to come to my wedding. She tried to leave him numerous times, and even flew to New Jersey once to stay with her sister for a while, but she always went back to him. We know now that these characteristics are typical for domestic violence situations. The victim gets scared and threatened by the perpetrator and they wind up back in the same place again and again. We also know that he would threaten to do things to her family if she didn't come back to him.

However, I believe this time she was very serious about leaving him. She was determined not to suffer any more physical or emotional damage, or to lose her son. She moved into the little white house at the front of the property and settled in. She loved it and it worked perfect for her and Trenton who was twenty-three months old at the time.

Although she was still timid and scared towards James, things seemed to be going well for her. She was doing everything she could to keep him happy and let him have Trenton anytime he asked for him. We spent a lot of time together after she moved back to Gilmer.

Cheyenne really wanted to go to church and so did I. She knew she couldn't go to the same church she had been attending because James would find her there, threaten her, and make her leave with him. He had already done it once before and used a family member to frighten and threaten her even more. Instead, we started attending a non-denominational church in Longview and I really liked it. I don't know if Cheyenne did or not, but I think she was content with anything. She just wanted Jesus without interruption.

As we were driving home one Sunday afternoon, just as we got into Gilmer I noticed Cheyenne tense up and she sat as far back as she could in the passenger seat, as if she were trying to hide herself from something. I could tell she didn't want to be seen. From the backseat Trenton started saying, "Daddy's truck, Daddy's truck!"

At that moment, I realized how serious the situation was for her. She was scared to death of James and knew if he saw us or knew we were anywhere close to him he would chase us down, no matter the cost. I don't think he saw us, but if he did, he didn't do anything that day. He turned the other way and we went on home.

Driving to church with Cheyenne after she moved back to Gilmer was a precious time. We talked and caught up on things, and really reconnected after she had been disconnected for so long. She would show up at our tiny little cabin (we hadn't moved yet) dressed in high heels. She was always so well dressed. I always wanted her clothes and I wanted to dress like her from the time I was a small child. She would meet me at the door on Sunday morning, always on time, smiling and very energetic about going to church. I could feel her excitement every Sunday morning.

One Wednesday night, about three weeks after she moved back to Gilmer, she jogged over to our house with Trenton in the stroller. While we visited, Trenton played with a baseball and rolled it all over the house. She didn't stay long. It was about a mile from their house, but the blacktop roads were hilly and it was getting dark, so Galen offered to drive them home in the side-by-side and she gladly accepted. That was the last time I ever saw her.

The evening of Thursday, September 26th, 2013, Galen and I were sitting in the living room watching television when the phone rang. Cheyenne had been shot and killed in the Gilmer High School parking lot.

James wanted to take Trenton to watch his two older half-brothers play their junior high football games. Cheyenne let him take Trenton and then met him before the game was over to pick him back up. She buckled Trenton into his car seat but as soon as she got in the car James began harassing her, trying to get her to drive him somewhere. She had experienced this too many times with James. She knew he was trying to kidnap her. When she refused, he pulled a gun on her. She tried to run away but she could not escape.

He shot her three times.

The first shot came through her shoulder blade from the rear as she was trying to run away. The second shot went through her jaw and neck which paralyzed her but did not kill her. After shooting Cheyenne two times from the opposite side of the car, he wanted to make sure she was dead. He walked around the car, cocked his gun, picked her up by her hair, and shot her in the head one last time.

This was the theory the District Attorney argued at her murder trial. It was absolutely gut-wrenching. I felt her pain, her fear, her loneliness, and heartache all in one moment. I hated it for my aunt who had to hear this about her daughter. I hated it for my grandmother who adored Cheyenne, the firstborn grandchild. I was beside myself for her brother. I despised it for Trenton who will one day have to hear the truth about his mother. I hated that a man could be so mad at someone to treat them like that.

I could feel James' anger as the prosecutor walked us through his actions that night. He had loaded another bullet in the chamber before shooting her with the third and final shot. That means a live bullet was already in the chamber before he cocked it, which caused the live round to eject and loaded another live round. The gun was a Glock 365, which automatically loads live rounds after ejecting the spent shell. He purposefully and intentionally loaded the gun to be certain he would kill.

With Trenton still buckled in his seat in the back of Cheyenne's car, screaming, James got in his truck and fled the scene. He called his wife, who was in the stands watching her boys play football. He told her what happened and told her to go get Trenton out of the car. When she arrived, Trenton was screaming and crying and all by himself. Cheyenne was lying in a puddle of blood, lifeless. Police came immediately. The football players were escorted off the field and into a safe location since no one knew who was firing or for what reason.

Little 23-month-old Trenton was fast asleep in my mom's arms when Galen and I arrived on the scene. We didn't get there until two hours after it happened. We came as soon as we heard, but everything was so chaotic that those who were there were too shocked to function and my phone had been on silent when my mom was trying to reach me.

My grandmother was one of the first people called. Cheyenne's mom was in Florida at the time and could not get home for another day or two. The ambulance was already there when my grandmother arrived, but they could not tell her what happened. For more than an hour she stood there thinking Cheyenne was going to come out of the ambulance and be okay. James was known to physically abuse her, so she thought Cheyenne had been badly beaten. In fact, she was recovering from oral surgery because he had recently knocked her front teeth out.

When they finally came out, they told my grandmother Cheyenne was "deceased." The lady who was with her when she received the news said my grandmother literally collapsed in her arms. She had to catch her so she would not fall to the ground.

We stayed up all night that night. We all went back to my grandmother's house and sat, shocked. We didn't know where to go from here. What were we supposed to do? Where would Trenton go? What would life look like now? There were so many questions and so much heartache. We loved Cheyenne and she loved us. We were supposed to be celebrating with her, not planning her funeral. We were supposed to be catching up with each other, not mourning over her.

Her wake was held a few days later. We picked out her clothes and made sure her hair was fixed just like she always wore it. When I walked into the room, my aunt Rhonda (Cheyenne's mom) was leaning down over Cheyenne talking to her like she was a little girl again. The back of her hair swayed from side to side as she passionately said her final words to her daughter. It was as if they were engaging in conversation and Cheyenne was talking back. Rhonda was crying, smiling, and conversing with her. She was probably telling her how much she loved her, how beautiful she was and how much she was going to miss her. More than anything, she was probably telling Cheyenne that we were all going to take great care of Trenton and he was going to be just fine. It was one of the hardest things I've ever witnessed. And, at the same time, I could feel the release and reconciliation between them in that moment. It was as if she was making amends with the future and what life was going to look like without Cheyenne in it. Rhonda was healing even through the pain as she talked to her.

There was only family there at her wake. Everyone was crying, even my husband who had only known Cheyenne for a few short weeks. He adored her gentle personality and loving heart. He knew her genuineness.

After the funeral at the burial site, I couldn't help but scream on the inside, "DON'T PUT HER IN THE GROUND!" I couldn't help but think about rewinding time. Going back, changing what happened. We were so close. She was with us just a few days ago! If only we could reach through a time warp and pull her out of it. It felt like that wall of time was still so close we could touch it. Putting her in the ground meant it was over. It was like a really bad decision that we couldn't get out of and the consequences were about to be handed down. There was nothing we could do, we were helpless and left feeling completely empty.

Chapter 10:

Chaos

The months after Cheyenne passed were total disorder for me. I had a baby at home, we were closing on our house and starting to remodel, I was a first-year teacher, and the family was in an uproar over Trenton; nobody knew who was going to keep him or not keep him. I got phone calls from family members just needing to vent, and then, I found out I was pregnant!

One day at work, I was craving a pickle in an extremely odd way. Someone jokingly, said, "You're pregnant!"

I pretty much gave them a go-to-you-know-where look and told them no way! I decided to take a pregnancy test anyways and sure enough, it was positive. I even emailed my midwife and asked her if there was any way I could be pregnant so soon. I breastfed for four-six weeks, only had one cycle, could I really have gotten pregnant? She assured me that I was most likely pregnant.

Cole was only five months old, and I could not handle this one. How was I going to handle two!?

After I took the pregnancy test, I didn't tell Galen right away. We were working on the new house and I didn't want to distract him with it that afternoon. I waited until we settled in for the night back at home. I was sitting on the couch with Cole. Galen was sitting in his recliner watching television.

In a shaky voice I said, "Galen, I took a pregnancy test this afternoon, I'm pregnant."

There was about five solid minutes of complete silence before he looked over at me and said, "Well, there's nothing we can do about it now. We are going to have another baby!"

The next thing I said to Galen was profound and, I believe, has set us up for where we are now in life. I told him I could not keep teaching with two babies at home. He didn't skip a beat, he simply replied with, "I know."

And that was that – I was not going to be teaching school the next year. I was going to be able to stay home and spend precious time with my babies!

In all honesty, I was relieved. I wasn't crazy about the thought of a 12-month-old and a newborn at home, but to know we were on board to welcoming a new baby was the first step. Plus, God knew, and we were moving into our new home in perfect time to welcome a second baby.

We moved into our new home right before Thanksgiving.

Things were still crazy with Trenton, the grief, and adjustments the family was making without Cheyenne in our lives. During those first six months, my mom kept Trenton most of the time. He went to the sitter during the day and she picked him up on her way home. It was something my mom was absolutely willing to do out of the goodness of her heart. We all wanted Trenton to have someone love him like a mother could.

Sometimes Rhonda would stay at my mom's house so she could see Trenton. Other times she would take him on the weekends. She lived in a house boat on the lake so it wasn't always safe to take Trenton with her. Sometimes other family members would keep him. We have lots of cousins that were willing to have him for a few days, but it was never consistent for Trenton. Someone different had him every weekend. Rhonda needed a break, my mom needed a break, and I wasn't much help since I worked and had a newborn. There were families that offered to adopt Trenton – everyone was willing to help.

The first six months after we lost Cheyenne seemed to drag on forever. During that time, I also lost an uncle (my biological dad's brother) due to a tragic accident, and my step-dad, Bill passed away just three weeks before we welcomed our second baby.

My uncle lost his life during an argument at home. His nephew had a gun in his hand when the argument started, and raised the gun to protect himself. When he did, my uncle began taunting him, saying things like "Go ahead, I dare you." My uncle finally came at him and the gun went off. There was no foul play, but it was heartbreaking. He was the main source of income for that family and my grandmother. He had a teenage son still living at home. He died on my mom and husband's birthday, January 25, 2014.

In May that same year, I got a phone call around eleven o'clock at night from my mom. She was slow to begin talking and immediately my heart went into panic mode. I knew she was calling me with bad news. I didn't know what she was going to say. When she realized I was awake and listening, I heard the words, "Daddy has passed away."

I was not expecting to hear that. My dad's health had been bad for a while, but I had no idea we would lose him so soon. He was about to turn 59 years old. Although he was not my real father, he and my mom were married when I was around four years old. I immediately thought about my younger brother and how heartbroken he would be. I thought about all the time we should have spent with him. I thought about the very last time I saw him. It was a precious time.

We were planning Cole's birthday party on my dad's birthday. I was even planning on having my dad his own cake there. We took him the birthday invitation about three weeks earlier. We visited him at his apartment in Longview, and he held Cole in his recliner while he rocked and sang to him. I have never seen Cole sit that still on anyone's lap. Cole kept looking up at him, completely intrigued, and my dad loved him too. He wanted grandbabies for a long time and he finally had one. Cole was the only grandbaby he ever got to meet. We gave him the invitation and I remember his specific words were, "If I make it that long." He knew he only had a short time left.

Bill was a big, tall man. He had dark hair when he was younger but as he got older his hair turned to gray and before he died it was almost silver. He was a team roper for many years and had one short thumb. He cut it off in the practice roping pen when he dallied off on the saddle horn. They were able to sew it back on but it was much shorter than the other. Because of his handicap he always asked me to button up the top and small buttons on his shirt collar. He looked like George Strait when he wore his cowboy hat and dressed up.

Bill grew up in a wealthy family, but money can't buy love. He was handed anything he needed and had charge accounts under his dad's name around town when he was a child. He never knew what it meant to go without. His mom was an addict and suffered from manic depressive disorder for most of his life. He told us that when she went to bed he would check on her and make sure she didn't burn the house down with her cigarettes. He even occasionally witnessed her shock treatments at Terrell State Hospital. He was an only child but lost a baby brother when he was very young.

Since he was handed everything on a silver platter and was never made to work hard for what he needed, he had a hard time holding a job or making money. He wanted to love and be the husband and father his family needed, but he was never emotionally stable.

The first time he fell and had to have hip surgery, my brother was in high school. After that, it seemed like one thing after another with him. Broken bones after broken bones. Health problem after health problem. He suffered from diabetes, he took opioids for almost the entire time he was married to my mom, then eventually got on methadone which was absolutely no better. His foot got infected and he almost died from gangrene once, and for about a year before he passed he suffered from congestive heart failure. He probably should have been on dialysis on a regular basis, but he was too proud. He never smoked a cigarette in all his life and I rarely saw him drink alcohol. I can probably count on one hand how many times I saw him drink.

We had a beautiful funeral for him and many friends and family came to pay their respects. We heard funny stories and stories that embodied who he was at his very core. Regardless of his addictions and downfalls, he would give you the last dollar he had in his pocket. Literally. He usually didn't have any money, but he was not afraid to hand it out. I know he loved his kids dearly, regardless of our disagreements.

A few years after he passed away, I ran into one of his previous step-sisters. She said he told her that of all his kids (me being his only stepchild), he learned to understand my heart.

That was very meaningful to me. He always treated me differently. I understand now, having an adopted son, how easy it is to take things out on them. It is easy to treat them unfairly. It is harder to love them unconditionally. It just is. I know many of you will be able to relate to that if you have stepchildren or adopted children. You have to work at it and you will destroy the child if you don't make that choice.

Thankfully, I never let his shortcomings change our relationship as I got older. We definitely had dry spells and there were times I literally cussed him out when I was in high school. But all in all, I couldn't hate him or cut him out of my life or take his grandkids from him. I just couldn't do it. I had been hurt by him many times but mercy triumphs over judgment any day. I wasn't even a Christian then and I knew that.

Three weeks after my dad passed away, Cason Miles Hutton was born. He was born exactly one year, one week, and one day after Cole – 111! It would take me almost four years to recognize the significance of that number in my life. God has an amazing way of showing you that He will never leave you or forsake you and that He was with you every step of your life.

Cason was a miracle child to say the least. We didn't plan him and in an unusual way he gave me a chance to redeem myself and everything I felt like I did wrong with Cole. What a difference a year makes! This time I wasn't naïve and I successfully nursed Cason because I put a lot more effort into it. I let go of little things like socializing. I focused on the needs of my children and recognized that being social isn't all it's made out to be. Even when we had friends over to the house on weekends, I was the first to go to bed instead of the last.

Something was dying inside me and I really liked it! There was a change happening and it was a good change.

After Cason was born, Trenton's babysitter wasn't working out any longer. I thought, "Well why not me?" I told them to bring him on over. Cason was not even two weeks old, but I figured it wouldn't be too hard. It was much harder than I thought it would be, but we made it through.

There was a lot of strife and division among the family still. Nobody wanted to speak up and lay it out on the table. I had many talks with my mom when she needed to vent. I had talks with another cousin who also needed to vent.

Sheron, a first cousin to Rhonda and my mom, willingly helped out with Trenton on the weekends. She and her husband were really considering adopting Trenton. Most of the conversations I had with Sheron were about Trenton and what my aunt Rhonda was planning concerning the adoption. Rhonda wanted Trenton to have a family and siblings to play with. The courts told her not to let anyone adopt him until the murder trial was over.

There were a lot of questions we needed answered about Trenton. I think we all had this idea that we didn't want to hurt Rhonda any more than she was already hurting. We didn't want to cause a bad day if she was actually having a good day, so there were a lot of "justifications" for not asking her directly. Instead, we talked amongst ourselves, hoping things would be resolved soon.

I remember one conversation with Sheron in particular. We were talking about Trenton, what was going to be done, who he stayed with that weekend, and anything else that we needed to talk about. I don't know how we got on the topic of James, but she said something that planted a seed nobody had ever planted in me before. It was a question that would pave the way for the King of Glory to come in!

She said, "I don't know that I have forgiven James yet."

That statement hit me. I hadn't considered that we hadn't forgiven him. I just kind of assumed we had. We weren't outwardly bitter towards him, we didn't talk about him, and we only thought about him when we were forced to with the District Attorney or if someone asked questions around town. Why did she think she hadn't forgiven him? I had even had a talk with a pastor about forgiving James. Surely I had forgiven him.

Chapter 11:

My Chains Are Gone

"His light broke through the darkness and he led us out in freedom from death's dark shadow and snapped every one of our chains." - Psalms 107:14 TPT

By the time Cason was seven months old, I was tired. I was looking for "something" and needed to fill a void in my life. I felt empty and wanted a break. I wanted to go to church. In all honesty, I needed a break from my kids and the noise. Galen loves to work, totally opposite of the dad I grew up with. He would work until at least 7:00, sometimes 9:00 at night in the summer, which was the time of year when both my kids were born! I had my kids all day every day and it never stopped. I had great help from my mother and in-laws, but it never seemed to be enough.

Galen agreed that we would find a church together. After many months of searching and visiting numerous churches, we agreed on one. It was a Baptist church not far from the house and was the church that Galen attended when he was a youth.

Many things happened during this time that caused me to question why others had faith in things I didn't understand.

A close relative was going through a family situation where they had to stand in faith on the Word and promises of God. This family member didn't approve of the situation. They stood for their belief, certain they were standing on the firm foundation of what the Word says. What was tricky is that the two families involved in the situation were Christians. So, why does one believe one way and another believe the other? With that going on, plus Cheyenne's murder trial just ending, tiny babies at home, and feeling empty inside, I was looking for a place to belong.

Our church was hosting a women's retreat. It was early May and Cason was just about done nursing. I really wanted to go and was excited to learn more about the ladies and build new relationships. I didn't really know many of the ladies yet and it was rather awkward for me but I pressed through all those unusual feelings. I felt very welcomed and jumped right into the fun activities and games. We stayed up all night and even when I did go to bed I wasn't able to sleep. I forgot my blanket and was freezing trying to wrap up in a small jacket all night! It was rather comical, I'm sure!

The next day, Saturday morning, we were getting ready for "breakout sessions," and one lady kept saying "Ask the Lord what session you're supposed to go to." She had complete faith and I was assured by her voice that God would tell me what session I should attend. However, I was wavering because I still didn't want to admit I knew nothing about the Bible or anything about Jesus. The breakout sessions were:

- How to have a quiet time;
- How to share your testimony;
- How to share Jesus with someone;
- And another I don't remember.

At first, I signed up for number three. I knew my grandad was in bad shape and I didn't know if he knew Jesus or not. I thought this would be a good way for me to learn the "best" way to dig into his heart and know for sure if he knew Jesus.

Inwardly, I thought that was the "highest class" so to speak and I didn't want anyone to think I didn't know Jesus or was on a lower level than some.

The morning started off with a group Bible study and teaching. We were going to break out after the morning session was over. As we sat down at our assigned tables, before we got started, someone asked me what breakout session I signed up for. I told her I was struggling with "How to share your testimony" or "How to share Jesus," but that I had signed up for number three.

She kindly responded with, "Well you have to have a testimony before you can share Jesus."

I didn't say much, just held on to what she said and then we started our study.

We had a paper in front of us numbered with questions and food for thought. We filled in blanks as we went. One question in particular struck me: "Have you ever been lonely?" Holy Spirit was working on me at this point and I opened my heart up to the truth. I felt the shift happen in my soul. I knew what I was writing down about loneliness was my way of letting go of my past, my hurt, and my guilt. I was facing reality and traveling back in time to those moments as a young teenager.

I wrote about the nights in my bedroom after having my abortion. I pondered on those nights and allowed myself to go back to that time. I opened my heart so my Father could heal that wound that was still festering inside me.

I had proud flesh growing over this infection for close to eleven years because I had not allowed that abortion wound to heal. Proud flesh is what grows on horses when you don't treat the deep wound properly. You have to make it bleed so the wound can heal from the inside out. When we had a horse with a deep wound, we would hook a spray nozzle to the water hose and spray the wound until it bled. It didn't feel good to the horses and they didn't like it but if you did not do this, proud flesh would grow on top of the wound, leaving scar tissue on top and the wound un-healed underneath.

When we finished the study, we began to talk amongst our table of eight ladies. They talked about their salvation. This church in particular (and many other Baptist churches also) put a big emphasis on knowing when you were saved and having it "nailed down." I remember saying to the table that I had always "known Jesus" and that I grew up knowing Him. I couldn't point to a particular moment when I was saved.

In my mind, "confessing Jesus" was enough. Nobody ever taught me what it meant to have a personal relationship with Him. I believed in my mind but I didn't believe in my heart. I knew Jesus died for me and that He rose on the third day but the manifestation of that belief had not taken root in my life.

In fact, I had recently watched the television series, "AD: The Bible." I remember the scene where Thomas said he wouldn't believe until he saw the holes in Jesus' hands and the wound in His side. Then Jesus appeared to him in the flesh! Jesus sat with the disciples and ate with them and fellowshipped with them after His resurrection. I was very deceived. I thought Jesus was more of a spirit after He died and rose again. That is the spirit of the antichrist at work.

> **"Here's the test for those with the genuine Spirit of God: they will confess Jesus as the Christ who has come in the flesh. Everyone who does not acknowledge that Jesus is from God has the spirit of antichrist, which you heard was coming and is already active in the world." – 1 John 4:2-3 TPT**

After watching that episode, it hit me. I realized that Jesus Christ was resurrected flesh and bone. His actual body was raised from the dead, not just His spirit. Jesus actually ate with the disciples after His death, burial, and resurrection! This was just one of the many misconceptions I had about Christ.

After confessing my "belief" in Jesus, one lady looked at me and without hesitation she encouraged me to pray and ask Jesus when and where I was when I invited Him into my heart. I took her seriously and was not threatened with what she encouraged me to do. It wasn't long after that we were called to get quiet and pray, or at least that's the way I remember it. I just remember praying myself, I guess everyone else was praying. I just knew that I needed to do what she told me to do and ask Jesus when I accepted Him. All these other people knew so I must be missing something.

I was sitting down in a chair and I bowed my whole upper body down towards the ground. I placed my hands over my eyes and covered my face as I began to pray. I asked Jesus all kinds of things. I asked Him what session He wanted me to go to, I asked Him when I was saved, I opened my heart up to Him about my abortion, I gave Him my hurt, my pain, my life, and anything else I could think of.

Suddenly, like a raging flood, faster than lightning, from somewhere on my right side, I heard an audible voice say to me, "Go, share your testimony!" Like Peter stepping out of the boat when Jesus called him to be a fisher of men, I was up out of my chair, headed to the breakout sign-up sheets on a table across the room. I looked at the lady who told me to ask and I quickly said, while continuing to walk, "He answered me!"

She smiled and I kept moving. There was a line of ladies already waiting to sign up, but I went right to the front, found my session, switched my name over and looked back at the ladies standing in line. They were all laughing and giggling, still trying to decide what session they were attending. God had so dramatically answered me that I didn't understand why He hadn't answered them. Why were they still wavering after two days about what group to go to? Didn't they know if they asked Him, He would answer?

Either way, I went back to my seat and didn't say a word to anyone.

I sat back down and started praying again. I went back to my same position with my upper body folded over at my waist, head facing down with my hands over my eyes. As I prayed, I heard the Spirit of the Lord say to me, "Because I have forgiven you, you must forgive him."

At the exact same time, I had a vision. I saw a link of solid metal chains, like you would hook up to tow a car or a truck. I saw them flash before my eyes and the middle shattered into pieces like a fragile piece of glass! It was as if hands from heaven came down and effortlessly pulled them apart! Other than dreams, I had never had a vision. It was the most clear and crisp voice and vision I have ever heard or seen, even to this day. It was an audible voice that nobody else heard. It was as audible as if someone walked up to me and spoke. It was not a whisper, it was not an inner voice, it was not a figment of my imagination. It was real, tangible, and life changing!

When you are dead inside and within a blink of an eye the Breath of Life speaks to you, it causes an awakening to take place inside your very soul. You are changed to a point of no return. It is the most exhilarating thing imaginable, yet at the same time completely discreet and personal.

Straightaway I had another vision and I saw myself fall to my knees and hit the ground. Although I was sitting in a chair in a room full of women, I was more in that place where I fell than I was in the physical room. I was in a dry desert place with what seemed like a cross in the background. It took my breath away and my spirit was abandoned to the Almighty God.

Humbled. I was humbled right then and there at the foot of the cross. I was knocked low, right where He needed me to be, reliant on Him and what He did on the cross for me. Not by my works or what I could do but by what He did for me.

I was free. I was healed. I was loved. I was forgiven. I forgave. I found my identity. I had a face-to-face encounter. I met Jesus Christ, Prince of Peace, King of Kings, Lord of Lords, Alpha and Omega, perfect love, chain breaker, and lover of my soul.

I was changed, I was different, I was the fire burning in a dry and desert land. The dryer the land the greater the fire.

I FOUND FREEDOM.

I saw people in a whole new light. I saw each person, especially James, as the child He made and knit together in the womb. I suddenly cried out for James's forgiveness and healing. I saw and felt God's heart for James and His heart for every human being on the face of the earth, whether they were murderers or Mother Theresa. I felt His yearning to set every heart free from hurt, pain, and shame; from every addiction, every bondage, every lie, and every unthinkable situation. He placed His heart in mine and I couldn't imagine ever letting it go.

When He said to me, "Because I have forgiven you, you must forgive him", it gave me His perspective. In the past, I had measured myself against others: I was better than some and some were better than me. Suddenly there was a counterbalance in my thinking. We are called to see people the way He sees them. He sees them through the blood of Jesus, putting the past in the past and not looking at their faults; addressing healing and forgiveness as He has instructed. We are to fight the hatred, anger, pride, and instability of the world with love for our neighbor, as we love ourselves. We must admit when we are wrong because if we can't do that, we are operating under a prideful spirit which is the "king of beasts" in Job 41. God is not a respecter of persons!

> **"Then Peter replied, "I see very clearly that God shows no favoritism." – Acts 10:34 New Living Translation (NLT)**

> **"For God does not show favoritism." – Romans 2:11 NLT**

God loves everyone no matter what they have done and we are called to demonstrate that same love. When someone mistreats you, consider it an opportunity to pray for them. When someone curses you, find a way to bless them. That's what Jesus said when He taught us to love our enemies at the

Sermon on the Mount (see Luke 6:27-38). These things don't come easy: we must grasp the truth of Jesus' words and put them into practice. Love wins!! Love breaks down the walls of hatred between us. The Fruit of the Spirit is love in all the various expressions: joy, peace, patience, kindness, goodness, faith, gentleness, and self-control. These things are love wrapped up into a perfect gift and there is nothing wrong with us using them anytime, anywhere! Love is your weapon if you want someone to apologize to you, to stop hurting you, stop bullying you or your children, whatever your situation may be. It is our reaction towards others when hate manifests that really matters in the battle. We have to trust God that when He says to demonstrate these love actions towards those who have wronged us, He will do what He says He will do!

Another shift took place when I heard the Lord speak to me about forgiveness. I suddenly understood that in the world's eyes abortion is acceptable, but not to God. He is the One who created this child in the womb and knew it before the child was even formed (see Psalms 139:13-18), and He was grieved over my refusal to give my child life. It was murder in His eyes, the same way James murdered Cheyenne. I didn't just take the one child growing inside me; I took out an entire generation and family lineage. Cheyenne's murder was gruesome and was a result of anger, jealousy, and bitterness and much hurt in James' own heart. Abortion came from believing lies, selfishness, and not seeing that God is my provider and supreme creator. I am not trying to be harsh or beat myself up by explaining it this way; rather, I am giving you a revelation of God's heart for His children. He hates injustice and death. He is Life, so the choice to end a pregnancy, to justify it with the word "fetus" rather than "baby" and to assure that it will not be born to life is absolutely one hundred percent murder, the same way Cheyenne was murdered with a physical gun. This is not my opinion, nor is it something that I suddenly changed my mind about. This is a revelation of Jesus Christ, who is the way, the truth, and the life. Nobody comes to the Father except through Him (John 14:6). If you want to be forgiven and walk in the fullness of the blessing of Christ, these are truths that we must accept and allow to be written on the tablet of our hearts.

Little did I know that what God spoke to me that day was actually scripture!

> **"Has God graciously forgiven you? Then graciously forgive one another in the depths of Christ's love." – Ephesians 4:32 TPT**

> **"Forgiving one another in the same way you have been graciously forgiven by Jesus Christ. If you find fault with someone, release this *same* gift of forgiveness to them." – Colossians 3:13 TPT (emphasis added)**

I was amazed at the change that had taken place inside of me. This time, unlike every other time I left church, I was different. Something inside me was real, concrete, tangible. I remember when I got home from the retreat and I stepped out of my car. The first person I really and truly confessed my faith to was my husband.

When I arrived home that afternoon, I stepped out of the car, looked at Galen and smiled. I don't remember if he said anything to me or not but I remember saying to him, "The presence of God was there this weekend." I knew from the moment I stepped out of the car and back onto my land that I was truly changed and couldn't go back to my old lifestyle and mindset. I didn't want to. The Hope of Glory was living inside me! How could I?

The most amazing thing was that after 27 years of yearning to understand and read my Bible, I could now read it with total understanding and awe. There was a new treasure for me to uncover every day! There was a new revelation just waiting for me to dig up. It was happening so fast. I was learning so much. This new freedom was something I had never experienced before.

Holy Spirit began taking me through Scripture to replace lies with truth. First, He taught me how much He cares for me. He taught me that if I will only seek Him, I will be taken care of, and that I don't have to strive for my needs to be met like the world has always told me.

> **"Look at all the birds — do you think they worry about their existence? They don't plant or reap or store up food, yet your heavenly Father provides them each with food. Aren't you much more valuable to your Father than they?" – Matthew 6:26 TPT**

> **"What is the value of your soul to God? Could your worth be defined by an amount of money? God doesn't abandon or forget even the small sparrow he has made. How then could he forget or abandon you? What about the seemingly minor issues of your life? Do they matter to God? Of course they do! So you never need to worry, for you are more valuable to God than anything else in this world." - Luke 12:6-7 TPT**

Then He taught me that He is creation itself. We can make plans, commit sins, or go our own ways, but ultimately, He will turn everything around for His good. He showed me that He is the Creator who knits every single one of us together in the womb. Even the ones who are conceived out of wedlock. Yes, even those who weren't "planned" were created and formed by the hand of the Creator who is omnipotent, omniscient, and omnipresent.

I want to leave you with some Scriptures as I close this chapter. Maybe you've had an abortion. Maybe you haven't had an abortion but you've done other things and now you feel crippled by shame. I want you to know that shame is not God. He does convict of sin, but it's always to either bring us into or restore us to relationship with Him, and He never uses shame to do it. The devil uses shame to drive us away from God. Don't let that happen! Meditate on these Scriptures and let the truth of them soak down deep into your heart and bring healing to those wounds!

> "You formed my innermost being, shaping my delicate inside and my intricate outside,
> and wove them all together in my mother's womb.
> I thank you, God, for making me so mysteriously complex!
> Everything you do is marvelously breathtaking.
> It simply amazes me to think about it!
> How thoroughly you know me, Lord!
> You even formed every bone in my body
> when you created me in the secret place,
> carefully, skillfully shaping me from nothing to something.
> You saw who you created me to be before I became me!
> Before I'd ever seen the light of day,
> the number of days you planned for me
> were already recorded in your book.
> Every single moment you are thinking of me!

How precious and wonderful to consider
that you cherish me constantly in your every thought!
O God, your desires toward me are more
than the grains of sand on every shore!
When I awake each morning, you're still with me."
- Psalm 139:13-18 TPT

"The Lord gave me this message: 'I knew you before I formed you in your mother's womb. Before you were born I set you apart and appointed you as my prophet to the nations.'" - Jeremiah 1:4-5 NLT

"Never! Can a mother forget her nursing child? Can she feel no love for the child she has borne? But even if that were possible, I would not forget you!" - Isaiah 49:15 NLT

Chapter 12:

Spirit of Error

"We [who teach God's word] are from God [energized by the Holy Spirit], and whoever knows God [through personal experience] listens to us [and has a deeper understanding of Him]. Whoever is not of God does not listen to us. By this we know [without any doubt] the spirit of truth [motivated by God] and the spirit of error [motivated by Satan]." – 1 John 4:6 Amplified Bible (AMP)

A week after the retreat, I was sitting in our young marrieds' Sunday school class. The teachers are a precious married couple, middle-aged with four adult children who all have grown up to serve the Lord. The wife began to tell about the week she had. The Sunday before, (the Sunday after the retreat) she began having symptoms of Multiple Sclerosis. She had had this disease in the past, and had been healed from it for almost ten years but suddenly, she started having symptoms again.

As she told the story, she mentioned spiritual warfare. She knew the symptoms she was having were not an actual sickness, it was warfare because she was healed of MS years before. She listed her symptoms which were shaking, rashes, difficulty speaking, and exhaustion, all tell-tale signs of MS. She called a friend of hers named Wanda, who she knew walked in authority and was educated in spiritual warfare.

They went to see Wanda for prayer. Wanda spoke to the spirits in her and began casting and calling out everything that had attached itself to her. By revelation and the power of Holy Spirit at work, this lady walked out of Wanda's office completely healed and totally delivered. She had not one single symptom left when she left that office.

As our teacher told the story, she really couldn't remember all the spirits that were mentioned but she did recall one, which is mentioned in 1 John 4:6

Of all the spirits she could have named that day, she only mentioned one: the spirit of error. When she mentioned this spirit, the Holy Spirit inside me quickened! That name caught my attention. I was all ears at this point and I soaked up every word she said. As soon as she said "spirit of error" a black shadow left my body, flew off to the left, and out of the room. I saw it with my own eyes as it faded into the distance. It manifested physically. I had just been delivered of a demonic stronghold.

I FOUND FREEDOM.

The spirit of error has many manifestations, including deception. In my life, one of the main indications of a spirit of error was the refusal to yield to authority. I was very defiant. From a very young age I did not like someone telling me what to do. I don't mean I got upset and cried a little. No, I became belligerently mean and angry. I would yell, curse, scream, cry, or manipulate my way around an authority figure. When I was little it was my mom. In school, it was my teachers and coaches. As a young adult, it was college professors or police officers; anyone who had the authority to control something in my life on some level. I even cussed out a landlord one time when I didn't get what I wanted.

I grew up hearing two stories about myself. I just thought they were part of who I was. It was my personality. I was just strong-willed. I know now that my behavior was the result of the spirit of error. One time, I was crying so bad and throwing such a fit in the store with my mom, someone actually approached her and asked if I was really her child. I was acting so erratic they thought she had kidnapped me! Another time, my aunt was shopping with my mom. I was acting up, so my aunt told my mom, "If you don't spank her, I will." My mom spanked me, and my behavior got much worse, so bad my aunt told my mom she would never ask her to spank me again.

These are simple examples and I am not trying to say that every person or child that doesn't yield to an authority figure is controlled by a spirit of error. We have to use discernment and seek God's wisdom on these things. He will reveal it and once it is revealed, it's done. Just speak to it and tell it to go. It is that easy and simple because it is not by our might or strength but by the Spirit (Zechariah 4:6)!

Another manifestation of the spirit of error is being unteachable. That was a huge one for me because I could not receive advice from other people. I only heard what I wanted to hear and argued my way around every conversation that didn't fit with my ways. I was too proud to ever admit when I was wrong. Christians in the church today are highly unteachable and not very moldable when it comes to God's ways. It was something I immediately noticed among fellow Christians after I was delivered. They were happy to talk about salvation and being washed in the blood but anything further than that, they just put a brick wall up. They didn't want to go deeper. They didn't want to face the reality that they had "junk" they needed to get rid of and receive true transformation. Every now and then a few leaders would be transparent and tell us what needed to change in their lives or what Holy Spirit had revealed to them about themselves but for the most part they only talked about sin and staying away from sin and what caused sin. They were very sin-oriented, almost to the point of making sin an idol.

We must stay teachable to the ways of God and chew on anything someone gives us. We cannot be scared to share with others the crazy things God is showing us. He is showing you for a reason. Share it! Don't brush something off immediately just because you don't agree or understand it. Chew on it and meditate on it through the Word and prayer. My mother-in-law, Kelly, said it best one time: "Eat the whole chicken but spit out the bones!" Take the word of God and what you hear from others as "revelation" and after giving it back to God, meditating on the scriptures, seeking God about what it is you're asking, He will show you what the bones are and what to "spit out." Even if you spit out meat, He will feed it back to you. Sometimes we just weren't mature enough to receive it at the time. You don't have to grasp everything all at once.

So many Christians today call people "false teachers" when in reality, none of us have full revelation and all of us are off in some way. A false prophet is really just someone who is not operating in love. These people are seeking to fulfill their own selfish desires even though they might be teaching truth. I think that would be a lot of Christians today! But what pleases God is our faith and staying yielded to Him.

Proverbs 10:12 says "Hatred keeps old quarrels alive, but love draws a veil over every insult and finds a way to make sin disappear." We read in Jude 9 that not even Michael the Archangel dared insult or slander the devil! It's not godly or in any way becoming to the Lord or the church as a witness to the world to argue, insult, or refuse instruction. We are not to call out false teachers, especially if we don't know them and don't have a relationship with them. Just pray for them and seek God about what they are teaching. That's not to say that false teaching isn't real – it is – but some of what is labelled "false teaching" might simply be a revelation that the unteachable don't have ears to hear or eyes to see because they are bound by the spirit of error. If you are bound, you will not know it until you seek God!

More than a year later, I got to meet Wanda and sit under her ministry. I asked her why I was delivered that day. Nobody laid hands on me, nobody cast that spirit out of me, and nobody talked to it and took authority over it, so I wasn't completely sure why it left. I had not talked to anyone else about it. I was still so young in the Lord I honestly didn't think much of it. I just knew I suddenly had a deeper understanding and a greater hunger for Jesus after the unclean spirit departed.

Her response was simple yet profound. "You had filled yourself up with so much Truth," she said, "that it didn't have anywhere else to go."

As time went on, I asked myself the question, "How did the spirit of error and deception get such a stronghold on me?" The answer is simple: I either opened a door through sin or it had a legal right to demonize me through the sins of my fathers. Through sin, a door was opened that allowed it to creep its way into my life. The sin can be as little as being offended or as big as having an abortion. I personally believe it had a right from the iniquities of my fathers because of the stories I shared with you about my behavior as a young child. I don't know and at this point it doesn't matter what door allowed error in – what matters is it is gone, and I know how to stay delivered.

The world throws so many lies at us daily through commercials, movies, social media, school, higher education, and the like. Before we know it, we begin to follow what the world says and never even think to ask the Creator of the universe if this is what He says is truth.

"Stop imitating the ideals and opinions of the culture around you, but be inwardly transformed by the Holy Spirit through a total reformation of how you think. This will empower you to discern God's will as you live a beautiful life, satisfying and perfect in his eyes."
– Romans 12:2 TPT

The second thing I know to be true about receiving deliverance is that once I forgave those who hurt me, my soul wound was healed. Healing and forgiveness are essential to deliverance. If you do not allow the wound to be healed, even if the spirits are cast out, they will come back seven times stronger because the door through which they came in has not been closed. They still have a legal right to your temple because God's Word does not give us any option on forgiveness. When we don't forgive, we are acting in disobedience to God.

> "When an evil spirit leaves a person, it goes into the desert, seeking rest but finding none. Then it says, 'I will return to the person I came from.' So it returns and finds its former home empty, swept, and in order. Then the spirit finds seven other spirits more evil than itself, and they all enter the person and live there. And so that person is worse off than before. That will be the experience of this evil generation." – Matthew 12:43-45 NLT

> "So humble yourselves before God. Resist the devil, and he will flee from you." – James 4:7 NLT

Ask Holy Spirit to show you where you are still harboring unforgiveness and wounds from your past (like trauma), and follow His leading. It might be uncomfortable and it might even hurt for a moment but the freedom and healing you will experience from it will be incomparable. You will wonder why you didn't do it sooner! This takes humility, but first we humble, or submit ourselves, before God. THEN we resist the devil and expect him to flee! From the day I was delivered, I learned every spiritual truth I could. I filled myself with the Spirit of Truth which is the Word of God. The Bible. It is alive because Jesus is "the Word made flesh" (John 1:14). Jesus is the Word and Jesus is alive! I began to see the spiritual battle raging all around me. My gifts, which are without repentance, were now highly active inside me!

When I read Ephesians 6:12 it all came clear to me:

> **"For we are not fighting against flesh-and-blood enemies, but against evil rulers and authorities of the unseen world, against mighty powers in this dark world, and against evil spirits in the heavenly places."**
> **Ephesians 6:12 NLT**

Almost everything we do is influenced by a spirit. We have the free will to choose to yield to the evil spirit or the Holy Spirit. We know that one-third of the angels fell from Heaven with Satan (Revelation 12:4). There is an army of angels and demons all around us (2 Kings 6:14-17). Praise God there are twice as many angels!

When someone is angry at me, my battle is not with that person. God dearly loves the person so I yield to love the one that's standing in front of me. The person is not angry, the demon is angry, using that person to manifest itself. When someone doesn't believe in Jesus Christ, they are not the one who doesn't believe, it is the evil in them that blinds their eyes to the deity of Christ (2 Corinthians 4:4). It is the hurt they've experienced or religion that has pounded them that has caused them to turn from God.

I am not saying every evil thing we do is a manifestation of a demon, but we need to use discernment and lean on Scripture that tells us we do not fight against flesh and blood! It helps you to see past the ugly ungodliness and into the beauty of God inside of them. God does not create evil. He is only good in everything He does. He is perfection and only creates in His image. He doesn't create the bad we see in this world. He doesn't make you an addict or give you a disease. We are the ones who yield to the evil and allow those lies to be planted into us, which will actually cause the natural manifestation.

Every day, I wanted to learn more about this. I waited with excitement and anticipation for the hour I had set aside to spend with God. I would put the kids down for a nap at one o'clock and then race outside to the shop, sit down at my little table and begin to devour the Word of God. I had a list of topics I wanted to know more about. Most of the time I would hear a single word that stood out to me during that week's sermon or during Sunday school. I would write it down somewhere and take that home with me.

The word "write" stood out to me during those first few weeks after I was saved. Holy Spirit would highlight that word to me and I knew He was speaking to me, telling me to write everything down that He spoke to me. I filled up notebook after notebook. I had spirals and notebooks and prayer books everywhere! It was hard to keep up with at times. Thank goodness, I am better organized now.

My life had changed, and I was changing very quickly. I was growing in what God had given to me (2 Corinthians 3:18). I was loving this "new creation" (2 Corinthians 5:17). I was young and still had a long way to go. I was a puppy dog jumping and slobbering on everything I could find. But I was growing, and I had faith. You cannot please God without faith (Hebrews 11:6).

I remember saying and writing the words "spiritual truth" down in my notebook. I used everyday events to explain what spiritual truths meant. One thing happening in the current news was Bruce Jenner changing his name to Caitlyn Jenner. Out beside Bruce Jenner's name I wrote "healing is the same for all" (1 Corinthians 6:9). Hurt is hurt, pain is pain and sin is sin, but God wants to deliver us – each and every one – from ALL unrighteousness. The hurt you feel from offense is just as important to God as the hurt experienced by a rape victim, and He wants to heal one just as much as the other. He is omniscient (all-knowing), omnipresent (always present), and omnipotent (all-powerful). He can heal both wounds at the same time, anywhere, no matter how deep.

What Holy Spirit began to teach me is something that the world cannot grab hold of: "We fight not with flesh and blood" (Ephesians 6:12). Humans cannot grasp the wisdom of God unless we seek it. He will give us wisdom on these things.

> **"Ask, and it will be given to you; seek, and you will find; knock, and it will be opened to you. For everyone who asks receives, and he who seeks finds, and to him who knocks it will be opened." – Matthew 7:7-8 NKJV**

When we learn to seek God and His righteousness, He will truly deliver us from every ugly lie, addiction, unrighteousness, and cursing tongue. We must submit our minds to be transformed into a new way of thinking, and only then will we walk in true deliverance. It has to get from our head to our heart, though. At the root, it is always a heart issue.

I used this example in the natural to explain spiritual truths and what Jesus was teaching me. Then, not even looking for it, I found the verse to back up what I was saying. I was blown away!

> **"When we tell you these things we do not use words that come from human wisdom. Instead, we speak words given to us by the Spirit, using the Spirit's words to explain spiritual truths." – 1 Corinthians 2:13 NLT**

If you don't understand or if you disagree with what I am saying, the next verse explains it even more:

> "But people who aren't spiritual can't receive these truths from God's Spirit. It all sounds foolish to them and they can't understand it, for only those who are spiritual can understand what the Spirit means." – 1 Cor 2:14 NLT

In Luke 12:54-57 Jesus rebukes the crowd gathered around him for not being able to discern the time they were living in:

> "Jesus then said to the crowds gathered around him, 'When you see a cloud forming in the west, don't you say, 'A storm is brewing?' And then it arrives. And when you feel the south wind blowing, you say, 'A heat wave is on the way.' And so it happens. What hypocrites! You are such experts at forecasting the weather, but you are totally unwilling to understand the spiritual significance of the time you're living in. You can't even judge for yourselves what is good and right.'" – Luke 12:54-57 TPT

We must learn to ask our all-knowing, God, who is love Himself, for wisdom! We can use logic or fight from our own human understanding to try and explain anything and everything we want, but we will never get anywhere.

> "For just as the heavens are higher than the earth, so my ways are higher than your ways and my thoughts higher than your thoughts." – Isaiah 55:9 NLT

Chapter 13:

Adoption

And you did not receive the "spirit of religious duty," leading you back into the fear of never being good enough. But you have received the "Spirit of full acceptance," enfolding you into the family of God. And you will never feel orphaned, for as he rises up within us, our spirits join him in saying the words of tender affection, "Beloved Father!" – Romans 8:15 TPT

Three weeks after I was saved, healed, and delivered by the blood of the Lamb, my aunt faced some serious decisions about Trenton's adoption. The murder trial was over, and she was free to make some permanent decisions for him. The District Attorney suggested that she wait until after the trial so there wouldn't be anything lawyers could use against us in the case. Multiple families offered to adopt Trenton. I know of at least three and there were probably more. It was a hard decision and a time of perseverance for our entire family, no doubt. It had been eighteen months since we lost Cheyenne.

Sheron and her husband were seriously considering Trenton's adoption. They were excited about it and it looked as if everything was going to be a go. One night at a birthday party, Sheron began telling me of some things going on in their lives and how she just didn't think they were going to be able to take Trenton. Her husband was considering a new job opportunity out of state, their daughter was getting older, and the timing for adoption just wasn't right for them.

This was a turn of events and I knew in my spirit, after talking to her that this decision now fell to Galen and me.

This sense was so strong that I called my mom before we even left the birthday party that night. In that moment I knew that we were supposed to adopt Trenton. I had a knowing. I cannot explain the "absolute" of that moment for me. It was an overwhelming, future-holding moment. Nothing was going to take me by surprise and nothing was going to stand in God's way of Trenton becoming our son.

After that encounter I started reading every single scripture I could find about orphans. I wrote in every inch of my journal what scripture says and God's heart toward the orphaned and widowed. God holds orphans and widows in the palm of His hand. He holds them very dear to his heart and watches over them with even more tender love and mercy because He is the Father Who fills the void and replaces the orphan spirit with the spirit of adoption (Romans 8:15). If God loves these children this much, why wouldn't we?

In those few weeks of seeking God about this decision, I never said a word to Galen. I only prayed and read, then prayed and read some more. I knew nothing I said would change Galen's mind or persuade him to adopt. Galen does not like to be pressured into anything. Pressure him and you can expect him to run the other direction as fast as he can. It had to be the Spirit of the Lord.

Sure enough, a few weeks later my aunt messaged us. It was the moment of decision for Trenton's future. When I received her message, I told her that she was going to have to ask Galen. I was all for it, but this had to be something he agreed to as well.

When Galen got the message, he came bursting through the back door from outside shouting, "What is this!"

So, I told him everything I already knew and had been praying about. I told him what I had been experiencing over the past three weeks and that I knew I couldn't say anything to him about it until it was time. I knew his personality well enough to know that I had to let this be his choice. It took him a full day to even process the information and this decision that was now before us.

Although this wasn't the first time Galen and I had discussed adopting Trenton, this was the first time Rhonda had formally asked us to adopt him. Galen finally called his dad. He sat in my car, not running, shut the door and just talked. I sat inside the house in the recliner and prayed. My heart was thumping, and my stomach was fluttering. I prayed for Galen's heart to desire this little angel in our lives. Not because we were the best fit for Trenton, not because he would have brothers to play with, not because we were the next of kin but because I knew Trenton would be raised to love the Lord with passion and desire. He would be raised to hear God's voice and be a walking testimony for others. We would raise him to not be lukewarm but a burning fire to be a sign and a wonder to the world. We were not called to raise this boy because we were a "good fit" for him. We were called to raise this child because he has a calling on his life and a book in heaven waiting to be fulfilled!

After at least an hour, Galen walked in the house, sat down in the recliner next to me and said, "We are going to adopt him."

Having finally made a decision, it was a relief to discuss Trenton's adoption. He was going to be stable, he was going to have a forever home. He was going to have security and someone to call "mom and dad." We also talked about what Galen's conversation was with his dad, Tim. One thing Tim said to Galen that changed his heart was about God's will. Sometimes we ask God for His will, we seek Him in prayer and we pray, "God, what is Your will?" The Bible tells us His will: it is for us to seek Him and His righteousness. When we don't hear an answer from God, sometimes we simply need to ask ourselves, "Is this righteous? Is this in line with the character of God?" God is not a God of do's and don'ts or rights and wrongs. He is a God of love, mercy, justice, and grace.

That was all my husband needed to hear. Adoption was the righteous decision.

"So above all, constantly chase after the realm of God's kingdom and the righteousness that proceeds from him. Then all these less important things will be given to you abundantly." – Matthew 6:33 TPT

After we sat in the living room for a bit, talking, crying, and trying to grasp how our world was about to change, Galen looked across the room at a picture that was ornately decorated with the word "family," and Trenton was in the picture; just him and Cole. It was a prophetic sign and confirmation to Galen that this was absolutely the right decision for us and for Trenton. He got up out of his chair and walked across the room, took the picture off the wall and handed it to me.

"Look at that," he said. I knew exactly what it meant. It was a sign of confirmation to us and it gave us peace.

A few days later, we sat down with Rhonda. My mom joined us. We discussed some of the logistics and different legalities that needed to be done for his adoption to become final. Before we left that night, Galen looked Rhonda in the eyes and said, "We aren't just doing this. We are excited about doing this!" My heart soared. I couldn't believe the words of love that poured from my husband's mouth. It was a very powerful and joyful moment, one I will never forget and that I know Rhonda will cherish forever.

Although adoption is very trying at times and there have been many adjustments along the way, that statement couldn't be more true. We were and still are in love with Trenton. I cherish the uniqueness he brings to our family. I admire his musical talents. I adore that he is very much like his mom and loves to be a helper. At the time of this writing he is six years old and has lived with us now for three years. When Cole was younger, I always said that he was supposed to have an older brother to entertain him. He was such a ball of energy and I was too selfish to put my own agenda down to do it all the time. He got exactly what he needed!

For a few months after the adoption, I had a recurring dream, four different times that I can count. The setting was different every time, but the situation was always the same. Cheyenne would show up in the dream, trying to get away. She was escaping what was going on or she seemed to not be where she needed to be. Yet, every time, Trenton was also in the dream, but he was never with her; he was always with us. I never really thought much about my dreams until I was attending Wanda's classes and she started teaching from the Bible how God speaks through dreams. One day in class, the Lord spoke to me about those dreams. I heard Holy Spirit say, "He's always been yours."

I've never had a dream like that again. Trenton was handcrafted, formed in the womb, and set apart for Galen and me.

He was pieced together with specific talents and desires to make our family totally complete. Only the wisdom and knowledge of God could know and orchestrate something so specific for us.

> **"Here am I and the children whom the Lord has given me! We are for signs and wonders in Israel from the Lord of Hosts, Who dwells in Mount Zion." – Isaiah 8:18 NKJV**

Trenton makes our family an Isaiah 8:18 family. We are a sign and a wonder to the world! Our story is being used by God to change hearts and set the captives free! To show the love of the Father and the forgiveness He has shown us. To proclaim to you that you have the spirit of adoption through the love of Jesus Christ. You are not an orphan, you are loved by the One true Father, the one who knit you together in your mother's womb and created you for His purpose!

Trenton wouldn't be the only child that became a sign that we were an Isaiah 8:18 family. There was so much more in store for our new family of five. Our journey was only just beginning!

Chapter 14:

My Freedom Walk

There's nothing like being on cloud nine with Jesus. This is how I felt for about six solid months after I was saved. We now had a family with not just two but three precious boys. I was so blessed to be able to stay at home with them. We were growing in Jesus and our family was now moving into a higher calling.

He is always calling us to come up higher. He is always beckoning us to come a little closer to Him. He is always quick to listen and slow to anger. He is patient with us and He is always willing to reveal to us His true nature and character. He is eager to give revelation as we hunger for it. I remember sitting at my "expecting place" one day. My expecting place was a little table I mod-podged and gave an overhaul. It had been revived just like me! It was perfect and sat outside in our shop. I usually went to my "expecting place" while the boys were all sleeping. On this particular day, a question crossed my mind.

"How are You going to be able to do this for the rest of my life?"

I was thinking about how much revelation I was receiving and how much I was learning about Jesus. I was learning a new truth about Him every day. I was receiving precious rubies from heaven. I was growing in him. My whole mind was different. My way of thinking was transformed. My understanding of Jesus was now something I was completely comfortable with. However, when that question came across my mind, it was like a switch turned off. I stopped receiving nourishment from the Word. I was suddenly trying to read it from my own perspective. I was trying to make a message out of what I was reading. My own thoughts were taking over, trying to make sense of it all. Things were changing, and I didn't know what to do.

I was very much like a newborn baby. Newborn babies don't have a set schedule for a few weeks. Then, about the time you get them on a schedule, they've changed and are ready for a new one. So, you organize your timetable to fit their needs and when you get settled into that, it's time for adjustments again! They don't eat at the same time, they don't sleep as often, and they get hungry more frequently. It's always something new and unexpected that first year of life.

It was the same in my life. My spirit was growing, and I didn't know how to change with the new growth. I was like a big Labrador puppy in its first year. Once, a boyfriend of mine got a puppy. That dog jumped on every car that came down the driveway, it slobbered on everything, and it wanted to play every second of every moment. She scratched me every time she saw me! Her feet were too big for her body and she was clumsy. Then, when she turned a year old, she was like a whole new dog. She was calm, she was obedient, and she knew her master's voice. She had gone through the process and learned patience and obedience through the training she was given. People that knew her previously wouldn't have recognized or believed that she was the same dog. She was different.

This was me. I had been so zealous for Jesus that I actually hurt people. Scriptures came to mind while I was having a conversation with someone and I would throw that scripture at them. Many times, I didn't know what to do with the scripture at all. Was I supposed to speak it out, hold on to it, what was the reason it was turning in my head?

If you are experiencing this or have experienced this before, I would suggest that is the Word, which is alive and active inside of you, guarding your heart from error and deception. However, don't speak them out unless you know for certain that it is a word from the Lord for that person. Those scriptures are to protect you, not for you to throw in someone's face. Quoting scripture at someone only causes arguments and hard-heartedness. That is not God's design at all. Use something in the natural, like a parable, to pull them into and explain the spiritual realm.

Around the time this question, "How are you going to be able to do this for the rest of my life?" came to my mind, I had become spiritually proud. I recognized that what I had been given was not given to many other Christians that I knew. Of course, what I had (and have!) is accessible to every Christian, but the growth I was experiencing was nothing like I had seen in anyone else. I knew I had something different, but somewhere along the way I forgot that none of this was by my works or by my might. Everything I had been given came from Jesus Christ and His shed blood on the cross. The only part I played was in accepting what He offered to me.

Pride is a very ugly thing. Job 41:34 says Leviathan "is monarch over all the sons of pride." He will attack those who are truly walking in humility. Leviathan is described as a sea monster that twists and coils. First, he will twist the Word of God. The serpent came to Eve and said "surely you won't die" (Genesis 3:1-7). She believed that lie. It's also described as a dragon in Job 41 and a serpent that coils in Isaiah 27. Carnal weapons will not defeat him. Only humility and repentance can defeat this monster. Admitting you're wrong and that you can do nothing without Christ will defeat it.

That time of trying to hear my Father's voice was the hardest time of this little Christian's life. To know the Father's voice, hear it audibly, get revelation every single day, and then suddenly nothing, was very painful. It was all because of pride. It was a making process. It was a refiner's fire. It was a growing season. Your hunger will determine the depth and height of your calling in Jesus. I was still very hungry and still wanted to know Him deeper. Praise God, He honored that desire in me! In the midst of all this, song lyrics came to me: "I know you've cast my sins as far as the east is from the west" by Casting Crowns. I really wasn't familiar with the song, but I knew it was Holy Spirit speaking. The lyrics were so clear to me! Then, that night, a lady said the exact same thing. She was even referring to the song and not the scripture. It was wild to me and I didn't really know what "confirmation" was at the time. He was trying to tell me to lay down my sin conscience, be dead to sin. It took me a while to understand all of it.

> **"So let it be the same way with you! Since you are now joined with him, you must continually view yourselves as dead and unresponsive to sin's appeal while living daily for God's pleasure in union with Jesus, the Anointed One." – Romans 6:11 TPT**

It took me about a year-and-a-half to get back into the full measure of hearing God's voice, and I will go into more detail about that in another chapter. However, I did start walking in a new measure of forgiveness towards myself. I learned that the Christian walk is not always easy and one little lie can take you down a very long, winding, and dark path. On that dark path comes a lot of guilt, weight you cannot seem to get rid of, and a lot of fighting in the flesh. Even though I was pursuing Jesus and loved Him with all my heart, I couldn't shake this heaviness.

I began trying to find more places to serve. I started looking for more things to do with the church. I wanted to be at every organized event the church had. I really wanted to serve on the "Women's Action Team," and finally, I did. I thought this was going to be a new way for Jesus to use me! I thought this was going to be good fruit for me. I was excited to get a chance to share how Jesus had healed me and set me free. I was going to minister to broken women and see them have an encounter the same way I did!

However, that did not happen. I served on that ministry for over a year and don't know that I ever sincerely ministered to anyone or saw anyone set free. They knew Jesus and loved Jesus, but they were still so bound. That was one of my giftings as soon as I was delivered from the spirit of error: I could see people's spiritual bondage. I didn't know the names of the strongmen specifically that had them tied up, but I could surely see that people were bound by past hurts and wounds and did not know how to get free. They didn't know the significance of holding on to unforgiveness, bitterness, strife, anger, self-righteousness, etcetera. I could see the sin in their lives that kept them sick and complacent but I wasn't knowledgeable enough to understand what I was seeing or how to teach them to move beyond it. I knew there were festering sores from their heads to their feet but I didn't have the wisdom to minister effectively in this area yet.

The one thing I did know was Jesus wanted to heal them! They simply needed to desire it and step into it. All that needed to happen was a prayer, a longing for Him to fill that nasty wound, hurting place, and seeping sore. I was so ready to see people set free but I didn't know how to teach others or how to minister using this gift I had.

When I was set free from the spirit of error, I was set free because I read the Bible. Hebrews 4:12 says that the word of God is alive and active, and sharper than a double-edged sword. Ephesians 6:17 says that the sword of the spirit is the word of God. John 1:14 also tells us that Jesus is the word that became flesh. The word of God and the words that we speak are very powerful. God created everything by just His spoken word. If you need deliverance, the Bible and the Spirit of Truth (John 16:13) will set you free! Allow it to transform your mind, lean on Him and not on your own understanding (Proverbs 3:5-6). Pray and open your heart up to the revelation of his word and begin walking in unity with Jesus. Jesus prayed for you and I to be one with Him as He is one with the Father (John 17:20-23). Hunger for more of His Word and He will reward you who diligently seek Him (Hebrews 11:6). Become addicted to Jesus and his goodness and replace the addictions of this world with Him!

I had been growing in my Christian walk and attending a church I dearly loved, but after some time I began to be subtly shut down by the leadership. I say "subtly" because it was indirect and truly, I don't think any of the leaders of the church meant to do it. They sincerely thought they were in the right. I started noticing that things I knew the Lord had given me were not being received, especially my revelation. I would say something and immediately there would be a comment from a leader that caused me to doubt what I was hearing from the Lord. There was no encouragement when it came to revelation

Finding Freedom

and walking with Him. After it happened several times, I began to think there was something wrong with me. and that I needed to quit talking. I thought maybe I was speaking out of turn or that, as a woman, I didn't need to talk at all. I even allowed scripture to be twisted in that way. That was not the truth. This was simply warfare that I needed to overcome.

The warfare was very real for me but mostly in my mind. Doubt was my worst enemy; not doubting who my Savior was or what God was doing in my life, but the revelation I was receiving and what I said was severely attacked after I spoke it out. The first time the Lord gave me an opportunity to share a message in front of a large group of ladies, I physically felt the demonic oppression come over me and cause me to hate what I just spoke. Someone corrected one word that I said "wrong." Because of that one correction at such a tender moment in my life, I was overcome with tormenting thoughts. There were months where I woke up and could plainly feel something wash over me. It was like a heavy weight was set upon my chest to remind me of all the "stupid" things I said. I even told God once that if this is what salvation looks like then I don't want it! But, God is gracious and He knew I loved Him and did not mean that.

Finally, the spoken word of the Lord came to me. I had been rebuking all kinds of different things into the sea but wasn't fighting the battle to win the victory. I was in my bathroom when I heard the word "oppression." I knew it was the word I needed. I immediately spoke to the spirit of oppression, cast it into the sea never to return, and began to walk out that battle daily. It wasn't immediate but……

I FOUND FREEDOM.

Chapter 15:

Surrendering the Secret

Although I knew I was healed and had no lasting pain or hurt from my choice of abortion, there was an eight-week healing study called "Surrendering the Secret" that I wanted to attend. At this point in my walk with Christ, I had shared my testimony to groups, told my family and even my in-laws about my abortion but this study was still something I wanted to do. I knew deep down that there was more healing for me, something I might not yet understand. I wanted to find that hurt because I knew that any hurt or ungodly thing that remains in us causes for separation from Christ and I wanted to walk in every amount of fullness that was available to me. Healing of any kind will only bring you more freedom in Christ.

This was about a year-and-a-half after I was saved. I met Misty, the lady that led the study, a few different times and she stayed in contact with me about coming. I met her first at Feminar the year after I was saved. She is the one who shared her testimony on the big screen about having multiple abortions and being healed and delivered from it through Christ.

I knew that I could definitely use more healing and expected this healing study to be good for me, and it was. I knew it would help me find a deeper healing than I even knew I needed, but I didn't expect almost every other woman to still be clothed with shame and humiliation. I hadn't realized how many women, and men for that matter, are not healed from abortion. I took for granted that every person experienced the healing power that I had at salvation, so I expected most women to be mostly healed from their wounds. I truly didn't understand how so many could still be walking in such guilt and shame even though they knew Jesus as their personal Lord and Savior. We even read other ladies' testimonies that weren't in our group. They experienced the same thing. They knew Jesus but had never been healed of their abortion. It broke my heart and I didn't understand.

I was in a group with about six ladies. Only one of us had multiple abortions. Some knew that they were pregnant with twins when they chose their abortion. One girl couldn't face her healing and quit after only two meetings. The oldest lady in the group had kept her abortion a secret for more than 40 years. She missed many meetings because it was so hard for her. She confessed that after our meetings, she would lay in bed all the next day because it was so hard on her. However, she was facing the battle head on and was ready to receive her healing.

I loved the healing study. I mostly loved the ladies and the fellowship and hearing their stories. I loved sharing how our weeks went and what we got out of the study each time. The week we finally shared our abortion stories was probably one of the most bonding and transparent nights we had. There were so many tears shed that night, tears of regret, tears of shame, tears of selfishness, tears of anger and hatred, but there were also tears of joy!

With about two weeks left, we were given a couple of assignments. We were to ask the Lord the name and gender of our baby and we were to bring a flower to remember them by.

We were going to have a memorial for them. Following is my written reflection from that day:

"Purple just seemed right. Purple flowers sit on my dining table and have reminded me of you all week. The week before, planning for your memorial, I wanted everything to be perfect for you. I wanted to dress nice, buy the best flowers, look pretty for you, and present myself honorably for you. When I arrived, only the two leaders were there. I felt awkward because the group was so small but pushed forward anyways. This wasn't about me, but you. There was a small chest for us to put our flowers in. I imagined that [chest] holding your small body, as your place of rest. The word "honor" is what I just kept hearing and thinking about. I wanted to honor you the way I honor Christ. I remember feeling so very selfish and wondering why this memorial was the "mountain top." This has by far been the hardest for me. I'm reminded of my selfishness even after I've worked through healing. We let the balloons go. I still don't know your gender. So, I let two balloons go. Pink and blue. All eight to nine balloons together at one time. Y'all were playing and dancing and being silly with each other. It really was a funeral service for you, my child. I still want to know your name."

I cried and grieved that entire week after we laid our children to rest. I never expected to be so emotional over it. I never thought I would recognize such selfishness in me. It really was a time for me to grieve the loss of my child after 11 years of holding it in. I was given a reason to grieve and I recognized the need to grieve so that I could heal even more.

The day the memorial was held, I went to the store to get a bouquet of flowers. I was in such a state of confusion and double-mindedness because I wanted to know my child's name but was also scared I wouldn't receive a name. When I walked up to pick out my flowers, there were some red roses labeled "freedom." It stuck out to me but in my state of confusion, I brushed it off as if the Father wasn't truly speaking to me. We were given the option to name our child, but I didn't want that. I wanted to hear the Father's voice. I wanted to know what He named my child.

It was about a week before I received the confirmation I needed. I kept seeing the word "freedom" everywhere and then, when I told the group that my child's name was Freedom, I knew that was the name the Lord had given me. Freedom stood for so much more than just a name. It also meant freedom for my family that didn't know the Lord. It meant freedom for me in a prophetic way that I wasn't expecting at all. It represented the freedom I found in Christ through giving up my abortion. And so much more!

But the name didn't help me with the gender. I was talking to the group about it and the leader of the group spoke up and told me that when we let the balloons go my pink balloon stood out to her. I had total peace and comfort in knowing Freedom was a girl and not a boy. I had a baby girl in heaven and her name was Freedom. Another sign for my family that we were an Isaiah 8:18 family.

I FOUND FREEDOM.

Chapter 16:

Deep Calls Out

"Let us go on instead and become mature in our understanding." – Hebrews 6:1b NLT

God watches over His word to perform it (Jeremiah 1:12). Jesus is the Word and that Word is alive and active in the hearts of His sons and daughters. It is by the spoken word of the Lord that that ministry and calling is birthed.

When I received Freedom's name, it was a birthing word that would call me into a deeper understanding of the Father's heart. Isaiah was given the word "Maher-shalal-hash-baz" which means "swift to the prey." He wrote the word down so witnesses could see it. Then, his wife became pregnant and when they had a son, God told him to name the child "Maher-shalal-hash-baz." God carried out that word against Damascus and Samaria. The name "Freedom" was a prophetic sign to me when I received it. I knew I would walk in a new freedom and calling. I also knew it stood for freedom over my family and salvation for all. It also represented the freedom in Christ I already had when He broke the chains off of me. After those years spent under tormenting, religious spirits, God redeemed me and set me free. It didn't happen right away, and it is still a daily process.

Two months went by after I received Freedom's name before I received another clear word from the Lord and scripture that launched me into a totally new atmosphere. A revival started near my hometown called the East Texas Glory Revival. Todd Bentley was preaching, and my in-laws told us to go if we could. They saw many miracles in a previous revival he was part of in Lakeland, Florida, one of which happened to a very close friend of theirs.

My soon-to-be brother-in-law was asked to play the drums at the revival. Funny how God orchestrates all these amazing details. So I went, along with my mother and sister-in-law. It was definitely a night I'll never forget. Nothing crazy happened to me, and actually, I walked away more discouraged than encouraged. There was so much happening that night and it appeared everyone was receiving something except me. During worship, all I could do was clap my hands. I had longed for spirit-filled worship for more than a year. Here I was experiencing it and all I could do was clap my hands! I wanted to let go, I wanted to dance, and I wanted to dive into what everyone else seemed to be experiencing.

I didn't let my discouragement get in the way, however. I kept going back. I wanted more. I loved the hunger that was in that place and I loved the confirmation I was receiving through the message. There were so many significant moments for me during revival, but some of the first things that happened to me made my spirit rise up.

"This is why the Scripture says, 'Arise, you sleeper! Rise up from your coffin and the Anointed One will shine his light into you!'" – Ephesians 5:14 TPT

I was sitting in my seat one night at the revival when the word "discouragement" was said. When that word left Todd Bentley's mouth, my spirit literally leaped up and my posture changed! It was definitely a "now" word straight from Holy

Spirit. Then, another night, he said the same thing. But this time, he didn't just teach on disappointment, he actually rebuked the birds of the air that can come down to take the seeds that have fallen on the soil through the open door of disappointment. He commanded them to fall out of the sky, so they can no longer come to steal the seeds that have been planted. Again, my countenance changed and the light was shining on the darkness within me!

Disappointment was where I let the enemy come in and steal the seeds that God was planting in my life! That's why I couldn't hear His voice, that's why I wasn't receiving revelation, that's why I was fighting so hard in the flesh! At times I would receive a revelation just to have it gone before I could get it written down. What Todd was saying was definitely real for me and caused me to evaluate my heart.

I also realized where I had allowed disappointment in. I was looking at other Christians and their walk instead of keeping my eyes on Jesus and abiding in union with Him (John 15:4-8). I was so relieved to have those nasty birds rebuked off of my life. I noticed an immediate change because everything God does is supernatural. We use natural illustrations, just like Jesus did, to explain what is going on in the supernatural and spiritual realms. Birds might not be the actual thing that was stealing my seed, but it was the agreement of the word that closed the door to disappointment. Plus, Jesus uses the birds of the air as a parable. He doesn't explain how or why they're allowed to steal the seed. In this case, it was disappointment.

As I kept going back to revival, new things were happening all around me. I was being awakened and revived and I was experiencing the actual manifest presence of the Holy Spirit come upon me from time to time. I was having dreams and learning the importance of spending time in worship. I kept hearing people at the revival talk about worship and how it ushers in the presence of God. They talked about worship being a weapon in itself.

And then, I had a dream and even interpreted the dream! It was confirmation that what they were saying was true. Worship is key. In the dream, my husband and I were being intimate. One of our sons walked in and said, "Is that your weapon?" When I woke up I thought it was the worst dream I ever had! I wanted to scratch it out of my mind. Then, Holy Spirit spoke and said, "Intimacy is your weapon."

I was blown away! I said, "Yes, Lord!" I will be intimate with You, I will love You, I will worship You, I will let You fight my battles and be my armor just through intimate relationship." I will never forget that and will always cherish the intimate relationship I have with Jesus, my Bridegroom!

One night, my future brother-in-law couldn't play the drums at revival, and referred them to my husband. Galen got a phone call from the pastor asking if he could play the drums with them and he said, "Yes!" I couldn't believe it. He was not only going to revival with me, but he was going to play the drums! This was going to be the first time for me to see him play with a band or worship team. Another orchestration by Holy Spirit Himself! That night was very significant for us because Galen came alive under that atmosphere as well. He began worshiping Jesus and singing praises to Him all day. It was so precious to me that Jesus would do this for us.

Meanwhile, we were still attending our church closer to home and were still involved in many things. At that time, the church was planning a city-wide outreach in the community. We were going to help those in need, do a Vacation Bible

School, build porches for some people, and other amazing things. I was super excited to step out into the community and be the hands and feet of Jesus. I was given permission to plan a garage sale through the church to help raise funds for the project. We already had plenty in storage to get us started, plus we made a day for those who wanted to donate their belongings as well.

We held it on two different occasions because we had so much stuff. On one of the days, a lady came in holding a little boy with a feeding tube coming out of his nose. As I stood there talking to her about him, the power of God came over me and I knew I had to pray for him! It was the wildest thing I had ever experienced but it was only happening now because I chose to GO to revival and be activated under the presence of God. I actually felt the Holy Spirit wash over me and surround me right then and there. I knew I had to pray for the little boy's healing. I don't know what happened to him afterwards, I just did what I knew I was supposed to do. I don't know what I said or how I said it. It was probably the most awkward and backward prayer I ever prayed. But I was obedient.

Shortly before we had the community outreach, I came across a verse that really struck me.

> **"So let us stop going over the basic teachings about Christ again and again. Let us go on instead and become mature in our understanding. Surely we don't need to start again with the fundamental importance of repenting from evil deeds (dead works) and placing our faith in God. You don't need further instruction about baptisms, laying on of hands, the resurrection of the dead, and eternal judgement. And so, God willing, we will move on to further understanding." – Hebrews 6:1-3 NLT**

When I read that verse I examined the church I was at and compared it to what I was reading in this passage and seeing at revival. I knew nothing about the laying on of hands and I sure wasn't seeing it there, but I was seeing it a lot at revival. I was beginning to understand that where I was serving in the church was "dead works" because I wasn't seeking first the kingdom of God. I was serving my church and people, not Jesus and what He had planned for me. I jumped into service instead of seeking and praying like scripture tells us to do.

Paul stayed in the desert for three years and told no one about his encounter with Jesus (Galatians 1:16-18). It also says "baptisms," meaning more than one. What other baptisms? I surely wasn't speaking in tongues yet and neither did anyone I knew at church. I found out later the New Testament talks about seven baptisms. I definitely never had a teaching on the raising of the dead! Eternal judgement? There was so much I needed to learn and I knew this verse was the confirmation I needed to move on.

There were still some things I was sifting through. Galen and I vowed to finish the work we promised to do with the church in the city-wide outreach. We wanted to honor them and follow through with our promises and designations. The first couple of days were easy because Galen and I were out building a ramp for a family whose young son was in a wheelchair. They were very grateful for it and the best part was I got to know her story, pray over her, minister to her, bind and rebuke things off of their home and land. It was amazing!

The next few days were very hard. Before, I would have been at church from dusk until dawn, serving and participating and talking to everyone I knew! Now, I could feel the tug of Holy Spirit telling me my time was over. I had to go home. I had to take my babies home. They were tired of being there and the new wine wouldn't fit into the old wineskin any longer. I could actually feel a wall set before me when I walked into the church that week and wasn't supposed to be there. I had to go home, I had no choice. It was the wildest experience. I never expected it, but I am grateful for the wall He placed in front of me.

Before this outreach started, there was one person in particular who always made it clear to us that we needed to pray about where we should serve; not just for this outreach but for all the ministries and different action teams they had. I agree with this to an extent. This kind of teaching taught me to hear the Father's voice, to press in and listen to Him, and to esteem His voice and plan for my life above my own.

However, that teaching became condemnation to me when I didn't hear anything from my Father. It caused me to pick up baggage and believe that something was wrong with me, or that I had sin in my life because I wasn't hearing from Him. It would really make me think I was inadequate because I thought God was always going to give us exact answers and tell us exactly what He wanted from us. In this case, I never heard where I supposed to serve specifically but I knew where my heart's desire was and I also knew that I wanted to minister to the broken and wounded. Thankfully, I didn't allow the condemnation to get too heavy that time.

I also noticed there were many young adults my age who sat under this teaching and kept "praying" about where they were supposed to serve. It took them until the day before the outreach to decide where they were going to serve. It broke my heart for them because I knew what they were going through and I wanted to tell them, "Just pick something and quit worrying so much!" They were so intimidated by the leaders they were under, they wouldn't even choose a place to serve.

We finished our jobs and followed through with our promises at that church. We even stayed a week longer because we were asked to teach a class one Sunday. Thank goodness we did, because I was able to minister to a girl our last Sunday there.

A song came on the radio a few days before our last Sunday and it pierced my heart. The song is called "The God I Know" by Love & the Outcome. It had been playing on the radio and I heard it for about the hundredth time but this time, it pierced my heart and it changed me.

> **If it was all about religion**
> **What to do, what to say**
> **What to wear on a Sunday**
> **All about perfection**
> **Black and white, wrong or right, never grey**
> **Well, I'd never make it**
> **I'd never be good enough**[8]

When I heard the words "Wrong or right, I'd never make it," I realized that Holy Spirit was saying, "Stop worrying about being wrong or right. You're never going to make it if you're so worried about doing the wrong thing. Just seek My face." All these petty decisions I was trying so hard to make "right" and serve in the "right" place had gotten me so far off track that I actually quit hearing God's voice because I was trying to hear

---

[8] Seth Mosley, Chris Rademaker, Colin Munroe, Jodi Rademaker, *The God I Know* (Nashville: Word Entertainment LLC, 2016), Lyrics retrieved from *https://www.azlyrics.com/lyrics/loveandtheoutcome/thegodiknow.html*

His voice. It made so much sense to me. I realized I was actually religious! I became the very thing I tried so hard not to become!

God is a rewarder of faith. You cannot please Him without faith. So, if you choose the "wrong" place to serve but you do it in faith, He will use you more mightily there than He will if you choose the correct place and continue to waver without faith. Don't hear me wrong. I am not saying that we should just go out and begin doing things even when we don't hear His voice. But I am saying that we cannot pick up condemnation or make it such a yoke around our necks when we aren't sure if we heard from God or not. Peter stepped out of the boat not knowing if he would sink, swim, or walk on water. It was his faith that allowed him to walk on water. What's also interesting is that Jesus didn't call him. Instead, Peter said to Jesus, "If it's really you, let me come and join you on the water!" Jesus' reply was "Come on!"

It was actually Peter's idea to step out onto the water and even though Peter couldn't handle it, Jesus still rescued him and calmed the storm raging around them. Jesus didn't come to this earth and die for us just so He could tell us exactly what to do all the time. He came to do life with us, to fellowship with us, to walk with us, to govern with us. It is faith that moves mountains and keeps the thin ice from crumbling beneath us.

The day we told our Sunday school class we were leaving, a girl came up to me and apologized if there was anything she had done to cause us to leave the church. This is the kind of condemnation they were carrying. I couldn't believe she thought that it could be her fault. She pointed to a specific moment when she said something out of line. I didn't even give it another thought. I jumped on the opportunity to share my testimony with her and what God said to me just days earlier.

God is not a God of right or wrong. She had to let that condemnation go. I hope it helped her and if it didn't then it was a seed planted in her heart that God will bring to fruition in due season.

Finally, we were free. We were free from condemnation, free from a controlling, Pharisee spirit, free to GO wherever Holy Spirit led us. We knew we wanted to go to Bethesda where revival was being held. We started attending and never looked back. It has never been about the church but about His presence and the hunger and fire that is released when worshipers arise.

I knew this was a God thing because when Galen and I first began looking for a church to attend more than three years before, one of the most important things to us was that it be close to home. Bethesda is about a thirty-five-minute drive for us both ways. I'm sure there are plenty of God-fearing people out there that drive further than that but for us, it was a lot. It was a step of faith that has so blessed us I cannot put all the blessings in this book. One thing I know for sure:

WE FOUND FREEDOM.

"But for you who fear my name, the Sun of Righteousness will rise with healing in his wings. And you will go free, leaping with joy like calves let out to pasture." – Malachi 4:2 NLT

Thank you for reading my book! I really appreciate all your feedback and I love hearing what you have to say.

I need your input to make the next version of this book and my future books better.

Please leave me a honest review on Amazon, letting me know what you thought of the book.

Thanks so much!

~ Cassie Hutton

Made in the USA
Columbia, SC
22 February 2022